SUSHI PARTY

KAWAII SUSHI MADE EASY!

KEN KAWASUMI

TUTTLE Publishing

Tokyo │ Rutland, Vermont │ Singapore

CONTENTS

How to Make Super Cute Sushi!

Decorative sushi rolls are cute and fun to make. If they are delicious on top of that, they are guaranteed to appeal to all ages! The key to making great sushi rolls is the flavor of the sushi rice, as well as the balance of the taste, fragrance and textures of the fillings, and this book will show you how to achieve this. Once you've mastered the basics, I hope you will experiment with sushi rolls made with the fillings you know your family and friends love.

Since raw fish is often used in sushi rolls, the basics of proper food handling are critical. Carefully read the food hygiene pages on pages 22–23 before starting. Then you can enjoy making delicious, safe and attractive sushi!

Why Make Super Cute Sushi?

They make both the chef and the diners happy!

Attractive to look at and delicious to eat, not only are decorative sushi rolls a special treat for the people eating them, they also make the person preparing them happy at the thought of the pleasure they bring. Try making the sushi in this book for everyday meals and bento boxes as well as for celebrations and parties, and put a smile on the faces of your family and friends.

You can have fun making them with your children!

Try making decorative sushi rolls with your kids! Even if the rolls they make are not perfect, heap plenty of praise on them for their efforts. Making and eating the sushi rolls together is a fun experience that is sure to create wonderful memories.

You can use decorative sushi rolls to express your creativity!

You don't have to stick to the ingredients used in this book. Come up with your own creative combinations, perhaps using local ingredients. Try creating your own designs for the sushi rolls, too. One of the best things about decorative sushi rolls is that they can allow your imagination to run riot.

How to Use This Book

The difficulty level of each item is indicated with stars. The more stars, the greater the difficulty. You can, of course, start with the recipes that appeal to you most, but before you begin, please read this page carefully.

A Guide to Each Page

Nori seaweed size

Pay attention to the length and width of each nori piece in the nori diagrams on relevant recipe pages in order to cut the nori to the desired size. The standard nori size used throughout is a half sheet, i.e. ½ a standard packaged sheet measuring 4 x 7½ in (10 x 19 cm) that has been cut lengthwise. When ⅔ or ½ a piece of nori is indicated, this is based on ½ a standard sheet. When a whole sheet of nori is used in a recipe, it is clearly stated "a whole sheet."

* See page 12 for nori cutting instructions.

Sushi rice

Sushi rice is made from short-grain Japanese rice specifically designated for sushi, flavored with vinegar, salt and sugar. All recipes in this book require a specified quantity of pre-cooked sushi rice. You can find instructions for making sushi rice on page 8. Sushi rice dries out easily, so it covered with a moistened kitchen towel or cling wrap.

Most recipes in this book call for sushi rice that has been colored or flavored. Specified coloring ingredients are mixed with the basic sushi rice to create a variety of different hues. At the head of each recipe the following information is given:

ⓐ The total amount of pre-cooked sushi rice needed.
ⓑ The amounts of different colored sushi rice needed, listed by color.
ⓒ The ingredients to add to the basic sushi rice to add color.
ⓓ The portions that each batch of colored sushi rice should be divided into for use in the recipe.

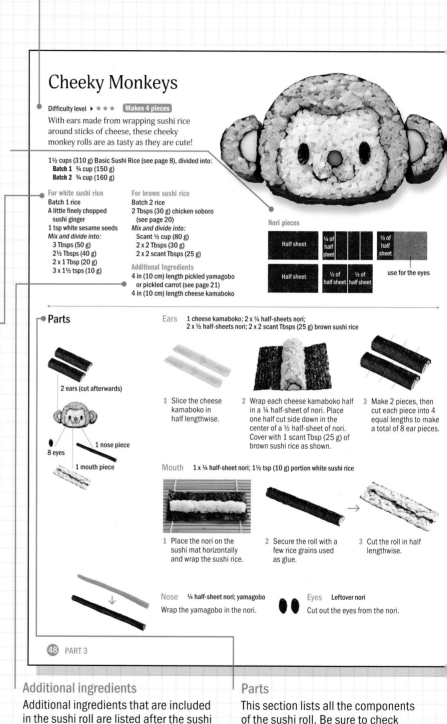

Cheeky Monkeys

Difficulty level ▸ ★ ★ ☆   Makes 4 pieces

With ears made from wrapping sushi rice around sticks of cheese, these cheeky monkey rolls are as tasty as they are cute!

1½ cups (310 g) Basic Sushi Rice (see page 8), divided into:
Batch 1 ¾ cup (150 g)
Batch 2 ¾ cup (160 g)

For white sushi rice
Batch 1 rice
A little finely chopped sushi ginger
1 tsp white sesame seeds
Mix and divide into:
  3 Tbsps (50 g)
  2½ Tbsps (40 g)
  2 x 1 Tbsp (20 g)
  3 x 1½ tsps (10 g)

For brown sushi rice
Batch 2 rice
2 Tbsps (30 g) chicken soboro (see page 20)
Mix and divide into:
  Scant ½ cup (80 g)
  2 x 2 Tbsps (30 g)
  2 x 2 scant Tbsps (25 g)

Additional Ingredients
4 in (10 cm) length pickled yamagobo or pickled carrot (see page 21)
4 in (10 cm) length cheese kamaboko

Nori pieces

| Half sheet | ¼ of half sheet | | ⅓ of half sheet | use for the eyes |
| Half sheet | ½ of half sheet | ½ of half sheet | | |

Parts

2 ears (cut afterwards)

8 eyes

1 nose piece

1 mouth piece

Ears   1 cheese kamaboko; 2 x ¼ half-sheets nori; 2 x ½ half-sheets nori; 2 x 2 scant Tbsps (25 g) brown sushi rice

1 Slice the cheese kamaboko in half lengthwise.

2 Wrap each cheese kamaboko half in a ¼ half-sheet of nori. Place one half cut side down in the center of a ½ half-sheet of nori. Cover with 1 scant Tbsp (25 g) of brown sushi rice as shown.

3 Make 2 pieces, then cut each piece into 4 equal lengths to make a total of 8 ear pieces.

Mouth   1 x ¼ half-sheet nori; 1½ tsp (10 g) portion white sushi rice

1 Place the nori on the sushi mat horizontally and wrap the sushi rice.

2 Secure the roll with a few rice grains used as glue.

3 Cut the roll in half lengthwise.

Nose   ¼ half-sheet nori; yamagobo
Wrap the yamagobo in the nori.

Eyes   Leftover nori
Cut out the eyes from the nori.

Additional ingredients

Additional ingredients that are included in the sushi roll are listed after the sushi rice ingredients.

Parts

This section lists all the components of the sushi roll. Be sure to check you have made all of these before assembling the roll.

Key points for spreading the rice

The basic method for spreading sushi rice on the nori is to place the nori vertically (see page 16). If you only have a little sushi rice, place the nori horizontally, as shown here, and spread the rice in the middle.

Adding more rice

These steps indicate the amount of rice to add.

Making a neat sushi roll

① Carefully read Part 1 of this book, "Basic Sushi-making Techniques."
② Carefully read the instructions for the roll you are making.
③ Gather all the ingredients you need (sushi rice, fillings) for the roll in the required amounts, as well as any tools you will need.
④ Make the small components. You can make these in any order you like.
⑤ Put the roll together.
⑥ Cut the roll.
⑦ Finish.

Face Half sheet nori; white sushi rice: 3 Tbsps (50g) ; 1½ tsps (10g); 2½ Tbsps (40g); 2 x 1 Tbsp (20g)

3½ in (9 cm)
3 Tbsps (50 g)

1½ tsps (10 g) 1½ tsps (10 g)

2½ Tbsps (40 g)

1 Place the sushi mat sideways. Put a half sheet of nori on top horizontally. Spread 3 Tbsps (50 g) white sushi rice in the middle, 3½ in (9 cm) wide. Place the mouth parts (2 halves) in the center.

2 Put 1½ tsps (10 g) white sushi rice on both sides of the mouth pieces so that they are the same height as the mouth pieces. Put the nose piece on top in the center.

3 Place 2½ Tbsps (40 g) white sushi rice on top and wrap it around the nose and mouth pieces.

1 Tbsp (20 g)

4 Place the sushi mat on your hand. Squeeze the mat from both sides to round the roll and place 2 x 1 Tbsp (20 g) white sushi rice portions formed into sausages on top. Make each edge stick out a bit from the sushi mat.

5 Wrap the sushi mat around following the contour of the indent, and close the roll while pressing the mat. Press so that the part of the face where the eyes will go is indented a little on both sides. Tidy the shape.

Assembly

Once the components are made, the roll can be assembled.

"Stack up in order" means to put the bottom components first and then build up the vertical parts in the order shown in the finished example. "Assemble upside down" means to flip over the main part of the roll and then add the remaining components in the order shown.

Assembly

2 Tbsps (30 g)

1 To make the head, connect a half sheet of nori and the ⅓ half-sheet nori together with rice grains on the edges, and place on the horizontal sushi mat. Place the face piece in the middle and put a 2 Tbsp (30 g) portion of brown sushi rice on either side to support the face. Make the rice about the same height as the face piece.

head
eye positions
scant ½ cup (80 g)
nose   mouth
Stack up in order.

2 Top with a scant ½ cup (80 g) brown sushi rice and wrap in a rounded shape.

Wrapping tips

The roll is shown in close-up before wrapping, so that you can easily understand the transition to the finished roll.

Close-up of the sushi mat. As a rule, the sushi mat is held in your hands and wrapped around the sushi roll, but some large, heavy rolls are wrapped on the cutting board.

3 Place the sushi mat on your hand and close the roll.

4 Shift the roll to the edge of the sushi mat and tidy the ends.

5 Cut into 4 equal slices, then add the eyes and ears to each head.

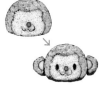

Animal-shaped Sushi Rolls ㊾

Cutting the sushi roll

If the roll is messily cut, the design will become warped. See page 17 for cutting instructions.

PART 1

Basic Sushi-making Techniques

This chapter has all the basics for making sushi rolls and scattered sushi, such as how to handle sushi rice and nori, how to color sushi rice, and recipes for Rolled Omelet and Egg Crepes and more. Make sure also to read the section on food safety and how to handle fish on pages 22–23.

Equipment and Tools

This is the equipment needed to make decorative sushi rolls.
Have everything to hand on your work surface before you start rolling.

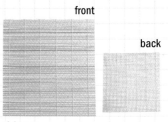

front

back

Handai, rice paddle and fan

A handai is a wide wooden container used to make sushi rice. Since the wood absorbs excess moisture from the rice, sushi rice mixed in it becomes shiny and delicious. The rice paddle is used to mix the rice rapidly in a cut and fold motion, and the fan is used to cool the hot rice. (See page 10 for a method of mixing perfect sushi rice without a handai, and page 11 for preparing it in a handai.)

Digital kitchen scale

To create neat sushi, it is essential to weigh the sushi rice carefully. Don't guess the amount, use a kitchen scale, ideally one that can switch between imperial and metric. Both measurement systems are given in this book, though the metric measurements (used in the original Japanese edition of this book) are more precise.

Sushi mat

The greener, shinier side of the bamboo mat is the front. Have this side facing up when you put the sushi ingredients on it. The knots in the strings holding the bamboo strips together should be on the far side, not near you, ensuring they don't get caught up in the roll.

Always keep the sushi mat dry while working so the nori doesn't get wet. If the mat gets wet, wipe it with a paper towel or kitchen cloth. After using, scrub with a kitchen brush to remove rice grains, and air-dry it completely before putting away. Never put a sushi mat in the dishwasher!

Knives and cutting board

To cut sushi rolls, long, thin knife blades are ideal. Use a dedicated sashimi knife, if you have one, or a santoku knife or a long peeling knife. Since sushi rice has vinegar and salt in it, it can corrode the blade of a carbon steel knife, so be sure to wipe it often as you work. I recommend a large plastic cutting board. Always use a dry board for cutting nori.

Ruler

Use a 12 inch (30 cm) ruler to cut nori or measure the rice fillings. One with both metric and imperial marks is handy as centimeters might be easier to work with than fractions of imperial measurements. Keep this ruler for use in the kitchen only. Don't share with the kids! Cutting boards with measurements are useful also.

Cloth

Thin cotton cloths called fukin are used frequently in Japanese kitchens. They can be purchased at Japanese grocery stores or online, but you can also use any thin lint-free cotton or cotton-linen cloth. Have both moistened and tightly wrung out cloths as well as dry ones to hand.

Using a dry fukin cloth

Using a moistened fukin cloth.   Rinse frequently to keep clean.

Use to wipe the sushi mat every time you finish rolling a sushi roll.

Use to wipe off any rice stuck to your hands.

Use to wipe stray rice grains from the sides of a bowl, or drape over the bowl to prevent the rice from drying out.

Use to wipe the cutting board.

Use to wipe the knife blade frequently. Always hold the knife with the blade facing away from you and wipe from the handle side of the blade upwards.

Making Delicious Sushi Rice

When enjoying sushi, the freshness and preparation of the toppings tend to take center stage, but the sushi rice that forms the foundation is vital to the overall taste. For the kinds of decorative sushi rolls in this book in particular, sushi rice is often the star, so be extra mindful of starting with and making the best possible sushi rice. Let's begin with rice basics.

Use short-grain Japanese rice designated specifically for sushi, and use only rice vinegar in the sushi seasoning. Don't use any metal in preparing seasoned sushi rice. Turn the rice out into a ceramic, wooden, or plastic bowl, and use a wooden or plastic rice paddle to mix the seasoning into the rice. Have someone fan the rice with a newspaper as you mix in the seasoning. The finished rice should be glossy and able to readily clump together, with a mild, "moreish" flavor.

Basic Sushi Rice

Although the rice used is specific to sushi, the cooking steps don't differ all that much from preparing regular rice. The main difference is that sushi rice is cooked with slightly less water to yield firmer rice. The instructions below are for using a rice cooker. If preparing sushi rice on the stovetop, follow the instructions on the package.

1 Measure the correct amount of uncooked rice into a bowl or container. Add plenty of water to wash the grains, then drain. Don't swish the rice around too vigorously, as it may break the rice grains. Rinse several times, draining the water completely each time.

2 Let sit in a strainer for about 15 minutes to allow the water to drain.

3 Pour the washed rice into the rice cooker and add an equal amount of water (1 cup of rice = 1 cup of water). If possible, let the rice soak for 10 to 20 minutes before cooking.

4 Once the rice is cooked, allow it to steam in the covered pot or rice cooker to fully absorb all the water.

TIP
Newly harvested rice contains more moisture. If you're using "new crop" rice, reduce the amount of cooking water by about 10 percent. The amount of soaking time needed will depend on the season: it will be shorter in the summer and longer in the winter.

Making Seasoned Vinegar

Seasoned vinegar for sushi is made by dissolving salt and sugar into rice vinegar. Always prepare the seasoned vinegar in advance. You can adjust the proportions of ingredients to suit your own tastes and those of your guests, as well as the type of sushi you are making. The tables on the opposite page provide measurement guidelines.

Adding the Seasoned Vinegar

The rice needs to be warm to fully absorb the seasoned vinegar, so it's important to add the mixture as soon as the steaming step is complete. Gently fold in and evenly distribute the seasoned vinegar without crushing the rice grains. Conventional rice cookers include the steaming step with the cooking time, so you can add the seasoning as soon as the rice is done cooking.

TIPS
- Let the cooked rice steam for about 20 minutes in the rice cooker or covered pot before adding the seasoned vinegar.
- Use a wooden rice paddle to gently mix the rice and seasoned vinegar.
- Quickly and evenly distribute the vinegar to coat every grain of rice.
- Cool with a fan when the rice vinegar has been thoroughly mixed in.
- Once the sushi rice is ready, transfer it to a wooden bowl or rice tub and cover with a tightly wrung out damp cloth to retain the rice's moisture. Use within 4 hours.

Sushi Rice Guidelines

It's best to make the seasoned vinegar in advance so that the salt and sugar can fully dissolve and enrich the flavor. The tables below show how you can vary the quantities of salt, sugar and rice vinegar (combined in advance and added after the cooked rice has finished steaming) to achieve slight variations in flavor suitable for different types of sushi. The plastic measuring cup included with most rice cookers is 1 go, a traditional measure for dry rice equivalent to ¾ cup or 180 g.

Mild Sushi Rice
For nigiri sushi, spherical sushi, everyday sushi, and sushi with strongly flavored ingredients such as vinegared or marinated fish

Uncooked Rice	Water	Salt	Sugar	Rice Vinegar	Yield
¾ cup / 180 g	¾ cup / 180 ml	⅔ teaspoon	2 teaspoons	5 teaspoons (25 ml)	about 1½ cups / 300 g
1½ cups / 360 g	1½ cups / 360 ml	1½ teaspoons	4 teaspoons	3 tablespoons plus 1 teaspoon (50 ml)	about 3 cups / 600 g
3¾ cups / 900 g	3¾ cups / 900 ml	1 tablespoon	3 tablespoons	8½ tablespoons (125 ml)	about 7½ cups / 1.5 kg

Standard Sushi Rice
Perfect for any type of sushi, including rolled sushi

Uncooked Rice	Water	Salt	Sugar	Rice Vinegar	Yield
¾ cup / 180 g	¾ cup / 180 ml	⅔ teaspoon	2⅓ teaspoons	5 teaspoons (25 ml)	about 1½ cups / 300 g
1½ cups / 360 g	1½ cups / 360 ml	1½ teaspoons	5 teaspoons	3 tablespoons plus 1 teaspoon (50 ml)	about 3 cups / 600 g
3¾ cups / 900 g	3¾ cups / 900 ml	1 tablespoon	4 tablespoons	8½ tablespoons (125 ml)	about 7½ cups / 1.5 kg

Sweet Sushi Rice
Typically used in western Japan, as well as for pressed sushi. Kids like it, too!

Uncooked Rice	Water	Salt	Sugar	Rice Vinegar	Yield
¾ cup / 180 g	¾ cup / 180 ml	⅔ teaspoon	1 tablespoon	5 teaspoons (25 ml)	about 1½ cups / 300 g
1½ cups / 360 g	1½ cups / 360 ml	1½ teaspoons	2 tablespoons	3 tablespoons plus 1 teaspoon (50 ml)	about 3 cups / 600 g
3¾ cups / 900 g	3¾ cups / 900 ml	1 tablespoon	4⅔ tablespoons	8½ tablespoons (125 ml)	about 7½ cups / 1.5 kg

Strong Sushi Rice
Best for vegetable sushi and in sushi where the rice is featured prominently

Uncooked Rice	Water	Salt	Sugar	Rice Vinegar	Yield
¾ cup / 180 g	¾ cup / 180 ml	⅔ teaspoon	2⅓ teaspoons	2 tablespoons (30 ml)	about 1½ cups / 300 g
1½ cups / 360 g	1½ cups / 360 ml	1½ teaspoons	2 tablespoons	4 tablespoons (60 ml)	about 3 cups / 600 g
3¾ cups / 900 g	3¾ cups / 900 ml	1 tablespoon	4 tablespoons	9 tablespoons (135 ml)	about 7½ cups / 1.5 kg

① Mixing sushi rice in a bowl

You can mix sushi rice with only a bowl and a flat plate that will taste just like you have mixed it in a wooden handai.

1 As soon as the rice has finished cooking, pour the sushi vinegar mix evenly onto the rice in the rice-cooker bowl or cooking pot.

2 Immediately transfer the contents of the rice-cooker bowl or cooking pot into a larger bowl. By turning the rice upside down like this, the vinegar mix that has pooled in the bottom will be redistributed through the rice.

3 Holding a rice paddle vertically, break down the wall of rice around the perimeter and mix rapidly, first in a criss-cross motion, then from the bottom up in a cut-and-fold motion. Repeat about 20 times to distribute the vinegar mix evenly into the rice.

4 Once the large clumps of rice have fallen apart, transfer the rice to several large plates and spread it out, working quickly. If you leave the rice in the bowl, the bottom will clump together.

5 Fan the spread-out rice to cool it. Fanning air in between the rice grains makes them plump and delicious.

6 Scoop up the rice on the plate from the bottom up to flip it over, and fan again. Once the rice has cooled down, transfer it back to the bowl and cover with a wrung moist kitchen towel to keep it from drying. Use the rice while it is still slightly warm, about body temperature.

② Sushi rice made in a handai

When you make five or more rice cooker cups worth of rice, having a handai (see page 7) is convenient. Wet the handai and the rice paddle and wipe off excess moisture before you start.

1 As soon as the rice has finished cooking, turn it upside down into the handai. Immediately pour the sushi vinegar mix over it.

2 Holding the rice paddle vertically, break down the perimeters of the rice first.

3 Holding the rice paddle horizontally, insert it under the rice and rapidly flip it to the left side of the handai.

4 Holding the rice paddle vertically again, push the rice to the left side of the handai to make space on the right side to cut and mix it. Turn the handai 180 degrees.

5 Holding the rice paddle horizontally again, use a cut-and-fold motion to crumble the rice, a little at a time, from right to left. When the rice has been thoroughly mixed, turn the handai 180 degrees once more and repeat the cut-and-fold mixing motion.

* This is all done within 2–3 minutes. If you keep mixing the rice, it will become too sticky and pasty.
* For more than five rice cooker cups of rice, repeat Steps 3–5 once.

6 When the rice is mixed, scrape the rice grains off the rice paddle and the sides of the handai with a wrung-out kitchen towel and gently flatten the rice.

7 Fan the rice to cool it.

8 Use the rice paddle to flip the rice over again from the bottom to cool it further. Fan again.

9 To finish, push the rice to one side of the handai. Cover it with a wrung-out moistened kitchen towel to prevent it from drying or absorbing any residual steam.

Preparing the Nori

Use crispy toasted nori seaweed to roll decorative sushi rolls. Refer to the nori diagram below to cut it to the right size. Store unused nori sheets in an airtight can or in a bag with some silicon dessicant to keep it dry.

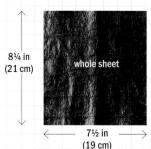

8¼ in (21 cm)

whole sheet

7½ in (19 cm)

Nori size for sushi rolls

In Japan, the size of a sheet of nori is generally standardized at 8¼ x 7½ in (21 x 19 cm). This is what is called a "whole sheet" of nori. While there are a few regional differences, most nori sheets you can buy in stores outside of Japan are the standard size.

Don't mix up back and front

Nori sheets have a back and a front. To make sure the front side faces outwards, be sure to place the nori on the sushi mat with the back side facing up.

The front of the nori sheet is shiny.

The back is dull and has a rough texture.

Most common nori sizes for sushi

The diagram on the right shows how to cut a whole sheet of nori with little waste. All the decorative sushi rolls in this book are 4 inches (10 cm) wide. This is almost exactly half the length of a whole sheet of nori. The roll is deliberately wrapped to be a little short so that it is easier to make and eat. This ½ sheet of nori is the standard size used throughout this book.

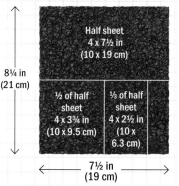

8¼ in (21 cm)

Half sheet
4 x 7½ in
(10 x 19 cm)

½ of half sheet
4 x 3¾ in
(10 x 9.5 cm)

⅓ of half sheet
4 x 2½ in
(10 x 6.3 cm)

7½ in (19 cm)

Cutting the nori by hand

1 Hold the whole nori sheet so the front (shiny) side is facing down. Fold the long side in half to make a crease.

2 Open up the nori sheet and flip it over. Fold along the same crease.

3 Once the crease has been folded both ways, the nori should split in half cleanly.

Cutting small pieces with a knife

1 Place 1 nori piece on a dry cutting board. Place the tip of your knife where you want to cut and hold it down with your other hand.

2 Still holding on to the tip of the knife, lower the blade in one motion to cut straight through the nori.

3 If you try to cut through the nori with the tip of your knife, the cut will be ragged.

Nori punches

Nori punches, available from bento goods suppliers online, are handy for small parts such as eyes and mouths. Keep leftover bits after making sushi rolls and use them for these small parts. Cut these tiny pieces at the very end of the sushi-making process so they don't get too moist.

Tips for Successful Sushi Rolls

For beginners who are having trouble making neat decorative sushi rolls, Chef Kasasumi offers these tips and solutions.

Problem 1

"My hands get covered with sticky rice grains!"
This is something every sushi beginner encounters. People with warm hands are especially prone to rice sticking to them. But the more rice sticks to your hands and fingers, the less goes into the actual roll, and while you're picking the grains off your hands, the nori gets limp and moist. It can go from bad to worse.

The quickest solution is to use gloves with an embossed surface, but if you're using your bare hands, try using "magic water"— also called hand vinegar (see page 14). Moisten your fingertips with this water-vinegar mixture and spread it on your palms and between your fingers. Then hold your four fingers tightly together when spreading the sushi rice on the nori.

A few grains may still stick to your hands, and if that happens just wipe them off with a damp kitchen cloth.

Problem 2

"Did I overstuff the roll? It broke apart!"
If you added as much rice as shown in the photos, it will be impossible to make a nicely shaped roll. The rice is piled too high in the middle and the fillings are sitting on top of the pile. Spreading the sushi rice too close to the edges of the nori can also lead to the roll coming apart.

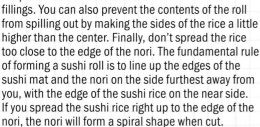

To prevent that from happening, keep to the recommended amounts in the recipe for both the rice and the fillings. You can also prevent the contents of the roll from spilling out by making the sides of the rice a little higher than the center. Finally, don't spread the rice too close to the edge of the nori. The fundamental rule of forming a sushi roll is to line up the edges of the sushi mat and the nori on the side furthest away from you, with the edge of the sushi rice on the near side. If you spread the sushi rice right up to the edge of the nori, the nori will form a spiral shape when cut.

Nori shrinks over time, so if you overstuff a sushi roll, sometimes the seams will slowly come apart. Moist fillings may also release water, so be sure to thoroughly squeeze ingredients that contain moisture before adding them to the roll.

Problem 3

"I can't spread out the sushi rice evenly. What can I do?"
Even if you've cooked perfect sushi rice, if you don't spread it out evenly, the resulting sushi roll will look messy and unappetizing when cut, and have an unpleasant texture. The best way to learn how to spread sushi rice is to practice it several times. Read the instructions in this book carefully and follow the guidelines, and spread a little rice at a time (see pages 14 and 16).

If you can't manage to spread the rice evenly, try moving rice from thickly spread parts to thinly spread parts by carefully picking it up with your fingertips. Never try to forcibly drag or push the rice along the nori, or you will crush the grains.

Here the rice is being pushed with the pads of the fingers. This is a no-no!

Problem 4

"When I cut the roll, the pieces are all different sizes."
The reason this happens is, again, because of the way the sushi rice is spread out on the nori. If the rice is spread unevenly and is of varying thicknesses on the nori, the resulting sushi roll pieces will be uneven, as shown here. The key is to spread the sushi rice as instructed in the recipe directions, and to place the fillings straight along the middle.

If you lightly press down the ends of the roll once you have rolled it, this will not only tidy the ends but help the contents of the roll to settle.

Tips for Making a Thin Sushi Roll

In order to roll up a decorative sushi roll skillfully, start by mastering the creation of a thin or regular sushi roll, from spreading out the sushi rice to rolling it up to cutting it. These steps are the basis of a decorative sushi roll.

Ingredients for 1 thin sushi roll (4-6 pieces)
Half sheet of nori (see photo below left)
Scant ½ cup (80 g) Basic Sushi Rice (see page 8)
Cucumber, 7½ in (19 cm) long, quartered, seeds removed since they can make the rice watery
Wasabi paste, to taste

❶ Place the nori sheet on the sushi mat

← 7½ inches (19 cm) →

Half sheet

8¼ inches (21 cm)

Place the cleaner cut edge on the upper side.

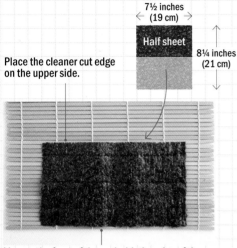

Line up the front of the nori with the edge of the sushi mat.

Use "magic water"

If you simply grab sushi rice with your bare hands, the rice will stick to them. "Magic water," or "hand vinegar," made by adding vinegar to a small bowl of water in the ratio 30:70, will prevent that. Always have some on your work surface. Quickly dip your fingertips in the bowl, then spread the moisture over your palms. This technique is used by professional sushi chefs. If you make your hands too wet, the sushi will also become too wet, so be careful how much you use.

If it is impossible to stop the rice sticking to your hands, try using gloves with an embossed surface.

Scoop up the sushi rice with your hands

Insert four fingers into the bottom of the bowl holding the rice, and scoop up the rice. If you take rice from the top, you can't stop the grains underneath getting smashed due to the weight of your hand.

❷ Spread out the sushi rice

Weigh the rice

Always use the right amount of sushi rice for the size of the nori. When you are just starting out, don't try and guess the amount but weigh it carefully. For a basic thin sushi roll, the amount of rice needed for 1 piece of nori is a scant ½ cup (80 g).

1 Form the sushi rice into a sausage.

2 Place the rice in the middle of the nori, a bit closer to the top as shown.

3 Spread the rice out to the edges using vinegar-moistened hands.

4 Spread the rice in this order:
❶ left near side
❷ right near side
❸ middle

Make the rice a bit higher on the near side, make a small indent in the middle and make the far side a bit higher to prevent the filling from sticking out.

for example, cucumber for a kappa or cucumber roll.

5 Put on the filling.

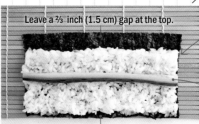

Leave a ⅔ inch (1.5 cm) gap at the top.

Leave a ¼ inch (5 mm) gap at the bottom.

Spread a little wasabi in the middle of the rice and top with the cucumber stick.

3 Roll up the sushi * The photo shows the roll shifted to the edge of the sushi mat for clarity.

1 Hold down the filling and start rolling.

Hold the filling down with your middle fingers, lift up the near edge of the sushi mat and start rolling.

Important!

2 Pull the sushi mat towards you to tighten the roll

Once the front edge of the sushi mat reaches the edge of the rice, pull the mat a little towards you to tighten the roll.

3 Lift up the edge of the sushi mat.

As you lift up the edge of the sushi mat, curl it back a little.

4 Slide the sushi mat to the front.

Roll the mat right around the roll

Holding onto the edge, slide the mat the width of 5 bamboo sticks to the front while rolling the sushi roll forward.

5 Tidy up the shape of the roll.

Flatten the ends, too.

Cucumber rolls (called kappa maki) are always made into a square shape. Press the pads of your thumbs onto the sushi mat on the near side, your extended index finger on the top, and the remaining 3 fingers of each hand on the far side, to form a squared-off roll.

- -

4 Cut the roll

1 Cut the roll.

Cut the roll in half in the middle with a sharp knife.

2 Line up the two cut halves and cut each into thirds.

* Thin sushi rolls are usually cut into 6 pieces. However, kanpyo (dried gourd) rolls are usually cut into 4 longer pieces.

The bamboo cut

Line up the two halves of the roll. Cut off one-third first, then make a diagonal cut through the remaining two-thirds. The cut side looks like bamboo, which is why it is called the bamboo cut.

Tips for Making a Decorative Sushi Roll

A decorative sushi roll is made by putting together pre-prepared components to create a design. For that reason, the nori used is larger and the amount of sushi rice increases, so you need to adapt the basic techniques used to make a thin sushi roll.

❶ Position the nori

Place the nori vertically on the mat as shown.

Line up the end of the nori with the edge of the sushi mat.

When spreading sushi rice on a small area of nori, you can turn the nori around so that it's easier to work with, as shown here.

OK

Spread on a few grains of sushi rice.

❷ Add another piece of nori

Most decorative sushi rolls are assembled by adding an additional piece of nori that's ½ of a half sheet to the base half of a half nori sheet. These two pieces are glued together with a few grains of sushi rice at the edges, with the sheets overlapping by about ⅜ in (1 cm).

½ of half sheet

Half sheet

Make sure the mat is completely dry before you put nori on it.

❸ Spread out the sushi rice

1 Put the rice on the nori.

When spreading out the sushi rice, do not press it too hard. Spread it out lightly as if you were scattering the grains.

In order to spread the sushi rice evenly, press it down first, then form it into a sausage shape and place in the middle of the nori. With your fingers, spread half of the rice downwards, then spread the rest upwards.

2 Spread out the rice.

Spread the rice in the area specified, and check to see that none of it is sticking out from the edges of the nori or if there are any empty spots. Fill these up with rice from other areas.

For long nori

Divide the rice into 2–3 portions. Place each in a sausage shape on the nori then spread out evenly.

Making the components ·

To make a decorative sushi roll, start by making the components or parts. To create a design, use fillings of your choice, such as egg, kanpyo (dried gourd strips), cucumber, pickles or other ingredients, as well as the sushi rice, and roll them up. Use a few grains of sushi rice on the edges to prevent the roll from coming undone. If the nori is too crisp and hard to roll, press it briefly with a damp kitchen towel or paper towel to soften it slightly before rolling. Once the roll is made, place it with the seam side down to secure the edge.

④ Roll

A sushi mat is essential for making sushi rolls. Besides using it as shown on pages 14–15 for making thin rolls, below are various ways to use it for making different kinds of rolls.

A A simple roll

Roll up in the same way as a thin sushi roll.

Small component rolls are made with thin pieces of nori. These can be rolled just with your hands or using a sushi mat. Either way, it's important to roll them securely so they don't fall apart. Very thin rolls are rolled with your hands.

B Rolling while holding

In this method, the sushi mat with the roll on it is rolled up while holding it in your hands. Place the sushi mat on your palm. Pull and roll evenly, a little at a time. The rice has a tendency to bulge out at the top the tighter the sushi mat gets, so press it down as you close up the roll.

Pay attention to how much pressure you apply to the sushi rolls from the top. If you press too hard, the design will be distorted.

C Rolling and rubbing

If you have a very thin roll with only a little sushi rice or very thin fillings, this method creates a neat, rounded roll. After forming the roll once with your hands or using the sushi mat, moisten the nori slightly and place the roll back on the mat. Fold the sushi mat in half and roll and rub it back and forth. This method is used to form several evenly sized rolls.

⑤ Close the roll

1 Make a "lid."

Add some extra sushi rice on top at the ends to ensure that the design is centered in the roll. Since it's used like a lid on top, this is called "lid rice." Beginners tend not to use enough of this lid rice, so it's a good idea to have some extra rice on hand just in case.

2 Overlap the ends of the nori.

If you are right-handed, hold the sushi mat over the roll with your left hand so that the nori on that side is stuck on the top of the rice. Open up the sushi mat on that side again, and pull the nori on the other side, holding it against the mat as shown, over the roll. Use a few rice grains like glue to hold that side of the nori down, so that it is securely closed.

⑥ Tidy the shape

Transfer the sushi roll to your cutting board with the seam side down. Drape the sushi mat over the roll and press lightly to tidy up the shape of the roll. (For a rounded roll, hold the sushi mat in both hands.) Press the roll on the sides with your hands or with a kitchen cloth to flatten them, and to settle the roll fillings.

⑦ Cut the roll

This is the last hurdle. If you can cut the sushi roll cleanly, the cut sides will look very nice. Wipe your knife frequently with a moistened kitchen cloth to remove any rice grains and move it back and forth to cut cleanly through the roll.

1 Make 4 evenly spaced marks with the tip of your knife along the roll. Insert the knife in the middle.

2 Moving the knife forwards, insert the blade into the cut up to the handle.

3 Move the blade back and cut to the center of the roll. Pull the knife out of the roll and wipe clean.

When you wipe the blade, be sure to turn the blade away!

4 Cut the remaining rolls in half, then holding onto both sides of a roll pieces with your fingers, cut into half again.

Egg Crepes

Egg crepes can be used instead of nori to wrap around sushi rolls. They can also be shredded and used as a topping, filling or mix-in. Adding some rice flour (joshinko) to the egg mixture, will make it easier to spread evenly. It will also become sturdier and less likely to tear.

Makes 3 fairly thick 8¼ in (21 cm) square egg crepes	
4 large eggs	1 Tbsp mirin
4 egg yolks	1 Tbsp sake
2 level Tbsps sugar	1 tsp salt
2 Tbsp rice flour dissolved in 4 tsp water	1 tsp vegetable oil

❶ Heat the oil and mix the eggs

Beat the whole eggs and egg yolks in a bowl. Add the other ingredients except the oil, and mix slowly with cooking chop-sticks so as not to make the eggs foam up. Filter the egg mixture through a fine mesh sieve. Heat a square frying pan over medium heat, and spread the oil around in it, wiping off any excess with a wadded up paper towel.

❷ Pour in the egg mixture

Turn the heat down to low and pour in a third of the egg mixture.

❸ Spread out the egg mixture

Move the pan around to spread the egg mixture evenly to the corners of the pan and cook it evenly.

❹ Peel the egg from the pan

When the edges of the egg start to look dry, insert a cooking chopstick and carefully peel off the egg around the side of the pan. Insert the tip and drape the egg on the chopstick as shown.

❺ Pick up the egg gently

Slowly insert the chopstick all the way to the other side. Then gently pick up the egg up.

❻ Flip the egg over

Put the edge of the egg closest to you on the far side of the pan the other way round. Move the chopstick slowly to flip the egg over.

❼ Cover with a sushi mat

After about 15 seconds, take the pan off the heat and cover it with a sushi mat, the shiny side facing up.

❽ Take out the egg crepe

Holding down the sushi mat, turn the pan over to remove the egg crepe. Repeat the steps above for the rest of the egg mixture.

Rolled Omelet

This slightly sweet egg dish is made of several thin layers of cooked egg, which are rolled into a thick, fluffy square. The layers must be thoroughly cooked before rolling them. Never take your eyes off the pan once you start cooking and work quickly to remove any air bubbles as soon as they form. Once cooked, the omelet is very tender, so don't try to lift it. Use your sushi mat instead.

Ingredients for 1 omelet
4 large eggs
2⅓ Tbsps sugar
2 Tbsps mirin
2 Tbsps sake
4 Tbsps dashi stock
Vegetable oil for cooking

❶ Heat the oil and mix the eggs

Beat the eggs in a bowl. Add the other ingredients, except the oil, and mix slowly with cooking chopsticks so that the eggs don't foam up. Filter the egg mixture through a fine mesh sieve. Heat a square frying pan over high heat and pour in the oil, wiping off any excess with a wadded paper towel.

❷ Spread the egg mixture

Turn the heat down to medium. Add a little less than ½ cup (100 ml) of the egg mixture to the pan, and immediately swirl the pan around to spread the mixture evenly to all 4 corners. Cook the egg.

❸ Fold towards the nearest side

Promptly pierce any air bubbles that have formed in the egg with cooking chopsticks. When the egg is soft-set, use the chopsticks to fold the egg 2–3 times from the far side towards you. Keep piercing any air bubbles as you roll.

❹ Rub more oil onto the surface of the pan

Push the rolled egg to the near side of the pan. Saturate a piece of wadded paper towel with oil and rub it onto the empty surface of the pan.

❺ Push the egg to the other side and oil the pan

Slide the egg to the other side of the pan and rub the wadded paper towel on the near side of the pan.

❻ Pour in more egg mixture

Add another ½ cup (100 ml) of the egg mixture to the pan.

❼ Spread the egg mixture under the cooked egg

Immediately swirl the pan around again so that the egg mixture spreads evenly to all 4 corners of the pan. Lift up the rolled egg so that the egg mixture can flow under it.

Repeat the steps from Step 4 onwards to make a thick rolled egg. Don't forget to keep popping those air bubbles!

❽ Lightly cook both sides of the roll

Once the egg is in a neat squared form, turn off the heat. Place a sushi mat on the pan with the shiny side facing up. Holding onto the mat, flip the pan over to transfer the egg to the mat.

❾ Tidy up the shape of the egg in a sushi mat

Wrap a sushi mat around the rolled egg, ensuring that the corners are squared. Rest the omelet to cool.

Glossary of Japanese Ingredients

Most of the Japanese ingredients used in this book can be found at Japanese or Asian markets or online. This glossary aims to describe unfamiliar ingredients so that you can recognize them, and to offer substitutions when you can't find the original Japanese ingredient.

Aonori powder is a variation of nori, where the seaweed is dried while it's still green and turned into a powder. If you can't get hold of aonori, use very finely chopped parsley leaves instead.

Bettarazuke is a rather sweet pickle made with daikon radish. It is available at Japanese grocery stores. If you can't find it, use an equivalent amount of finely minced sweet pickled white onion (drain well before adding to rice).

Cheese Kamaboko see **Kamaboko**

Chicken soboro is finely ground chicken cooked with soy sauce, sake and sugar. It's used in this book to make brown sushi rice. This recipe is for a 1½ cup (180 g) portion that can be refrigerated for 2–3 days or frozen for up to a month and used as needed: In a small pan, combine 1½ cups (180 g) finely ground chicken, 2 tablespoons soy sauce, 1 tablespoon sake and 2 tablespoons sugar. Cook over medium heat stirring constantly so no clumps form, until there is no liquid left in the pan.

Chikuwa is a sausage-shaped fish-paste product with a hole in the middle. It is usually brown on the outside since it's grilled. Chikuwa is available at Japanese grocery stores.

Cucumber used in this book is Japanese cucumber, which is smaller than English cucumber, with thin skin and underdeveloped seeds. Substitute skinned and deseeded English cucumber if necessary.

Deep-fried tofu pockets are used to stuff with sushi rice to make the kind of sushi called inarizushi in Japanese. Ready-made inarizushi skins are available in vacuum packs in Japanese or general Asian grocery stores. Canned inarizushi skins are also available, but should only be used if no other alternatives are available, since they are usually not very good quality.

Eel is called for to make Cute Helicopters on page 68. This recipe uses eel kabayaki, eel cooked in a salty-sweet sauce, available vacuum packed from Japanese groceries.

Fish sausage is made with ground white fish. Similar to kamaboko, it has a light pink color. It is available at well-stocked Japanese grocery stores. Finely textured frankfurters or wiener sausages can be substituted.

Flying fish roe, called tobiko in Japanese, are tiny fish eggs that have been brined and often colored with some food coloring. The natural color is a pale yellow, but the most commonly seen color is orange-red. Green tobiko is often flavored with a little wasabi, but not enough to be too sharp. It's available at Japanese grocery stores, fresh or frozen. For an orange tobiko substitute try using carrot: Grate ⅓ cup (35 g) carrot with a microplane or fine grater. Sprinkle with ½ tsp salt and 1 tsp lemon juice, and mix well. Let stand for 5 minutes then squeeze well to remove as much moisture as possible before adding to sushi rice.

Ikura is salmon roe that has been marinated in a soy sauce based mixture. Salmon caviar, which treats the eggs in a brine, can be used too. Salmon caviar is widely available, and ikura is available at Japanese grocery stores.

Kamaboko is a firm, slightly rubbery fish cake. It usually comes in a dome shape on top of a small piece of wood, but it is also sold in a square shape. It is sometimes dyed a light pink with food coloring. Cheese kamaboko is a light yellow, sausage-shaped product made with white fish paste and cheese. Both are available at Japanese grocery stores. For tiny parts on decorative sushi, try substituting processed cheese or cheese sticks if you can't find kamaboko or cheese kamaboko.

Kanpyo are dried gourd strips that have been soaked in water and cooked in a sweet-savory sauce. Precooked kanpyo are available at Japanese grocery stores. If you can't find kanpyo, substitute any long, thinly sliced crunchy vegetable that can be eaten raw.

Mentaiko is pollock roe marinated in a chili pepper sauce, which imparts a spicy flavor and bright red color. If you can't find any, substitute very finely chopped sundried tomatoes cured in olive oil, with a pinch of crushed or powdered red pepper.

Mitsuba is a green herb, sometimes called Japanese parsley. Italian or flat-leaf parsley can be substituted in a pinch if used as a decorative element.

Nozawana-zuke is a preserved food or pickle made by drying and salting a green vegetable called nozawana. It is available at well stocked Japanese grocery stores. If you can't find it, substitute with spinach prepared as follows: Add 2 Tbsps salt to 1 quart (1 liter) water, bring to a boil and blanch 2 cups (60 g) spinach leaves for 30 seconds. Drain and squeeze to remove as much moisture as possible before mixing with sushi rice. If a recipe calls for nozawana-zuke stems, you can substitute thin Swiss chard or spinach stems, blanched in heavily salted water and drained well.

Oboro is flaked and cooked white fish that is dyed a pale pink with food coloring. Denbu is a similar product, but is usually a lot darker pink in color and is much sweeter. Oboro is available at Japanese grocery stores. If you can't get hold of it, you can add a pink color to your sushi with a small amount of finely grated beet (use a microplane if possible): Grate ⅓ cup raw beet and season with ¼ teaspoon salt, stir to mix, and let stand for 5 minutes. Drain well and use as needed. Store refrigerated for up to a week. Use ¼ tsp beet per ½ cup (100 g) sushi rice.

Red pickled ginger is called *beni-shoga* in Japanese, and is used as a topping or garnish for many types of Japanese dish. It has a deep red color. Can be found in Japanese grocery stores and many regular supermarkets.

Shiso leaves can be found at well stocked Japanese grocery stores. The recipes in this book use the green variety, not the purple ones.

Sushi ginger is called *gari* in Japanese. This is the thin-sliced very pale pink-yellow ginger that is served with sushi. You can find it in Japanese grocery stores and many regular supermarkets.

Takuan is pickled daikon radish, and is sold either yellow or white. The most popular Japanese pickle, it is widely available in Asian supermarkets and in the macrobiotic section of health-food stores. If you can't find it, substitute chopped pickled carrots or cauliflower from a pickled Italian vegetable mix, making sure to drain well before adding to sushi rice.

Tarako is salted cod roe, similar to mentaiko, but not spicy. Available at Japanese grocery stores.

Tofu see **Deep-fried tofu pockets**

Umeboshi plum paste. Available in tubes or bottles in Asian markets.

Yamagobo is a type of burdock root. Pickled yamagobo, a standard ingredient in sushi rolls, is available at Japanese grocery stores. If you can't find it, substitute pickled carrot: Peel and thinly slice a medium carrot. Bring ½ cup (120 ml) rice vinegar, 1 teaspoon salt, and 1½ tablespoons sugar to a boil in a small pan. Pour the hot vinegar over the carrot slices and leave to cool. Refrigerate in a closed container for up to a week.

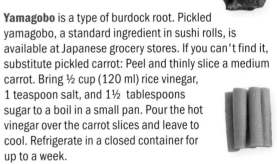

Yukari is a salty, slightly sour powder made with the red or purple shiso leaves that are used to make umeboshi plums. It's available at Japanese grocery stores or online. If you can't find yukari, substitute an equivalent amount of umeboshi plum paste or finely chopped umeboshi pickled plum.

Don't forget to note any allergenic foods. Eggs, kamaboko, salmon roe and other ingredients commonly used in sushi are recognized as being allergenic foods. In addition, ready-made foods used in sushi may contain allergens you are not aware of. For instance, oboro usually contains egg whites. When serving sushi rolls at parties and so on, be sure to let your guests know about the ingredients.

Three basic rules for preventing food poisoning
Don't add bacteria. Don't increase bacteria. Eliminate bacteria.

SAFETY TIPS!

When you are making sushi, you are often handling raw fish , so you must pay attention to good hygiene. To prevent food poisoning, the three rules above are critical. Here are the basics of correct food handling.

1: Always work with clean hands
Start every sushi making session by washing your hands. Take off any jewelry or watches. Was the areas between your fingers and around your thumbs well. Keep the handle of the water faucet clean, to avoid secondary contamination. If you use gloves, keep them strictly for use with food and cooking equipment. Change to new gloves after making sushi with raw fish.

2: Wash and disinfect your kitchen tools
Simply rinsing your cutting board and knives after cutting meat or fish, then cutting vegetables or sushi rolls with the same equipment, is very likely to cause food poisoning. Either use separate cutting boards for prepping food and finishing it, or flip your cutting board over for each task. (Consider using separate boards for meat and fish, and for vegetables.) Wash your kitchen tools with a clean sponge using dishwashing detergent, and disinfect them using boiling water, disinfecting solution or sprays. Bacteria can multiply in water left clinging to washed bowls and other containers, so be sure to dry them properly.

Knives are just as likely as cutting boards to have secondary contamination. Make sure to wash them properly after each use.

Use separate kitchen cloths for wiping dishes, prepping food and cooking food. Change them frequently and disinfect by boiling or soaking in a bleach solution.

Scrub off any rice grains stuck on a sushi mat using a dishwashing brush or tawashi scrubber. Dry the mat thoroughly before storing or it may become moldy.

3: Avoid the dangerous temperature of 50–140°F (10–60°C)
Never leave ingredients or finished food at a temperature where bacteria and microbes are most likely to increase. Store ingredients at a temperature that is as low as possible without freezing. If you don't have access to a cool refrigerator, use an insulated container with an ice pack. Always check the temperature of your refrigerator, which should be kept at 35.6 to 46.4°F (2 to 8°C). Your freezer should be kept at −8 to 0°F (−18 to −22°C). Keep the handles and inside of the refrigerator and freezer clean and disinfected.

4: Do not cook when you are unwell
Never cook when you have digestive problems, a fever or a cough, or cuts on your hands. Bandages are breeding grounds for bacteria, as is broken skin. Taking care of your health is also a critical part of maintaining good hygiene.

5: Make sure everyone knows how long something keeps
If you are conducting sushi-making classes and your students take home what they've made, let them know the expiry date for each ingredient. If someone gets food poisoning, even if the ultimate responsibility is with the maker of that food, the one who prepped the ingredients beforehand (you) will bear some responsibility too. It's important to prep and store the ingredients properly, and the teacher of a cooking class must have the correct knowledge about proper food handling.

Beware of the Big Six Causes of Food Poisoning!

● **Vibrio parahaemolyticus** This bacterium lives in sea water and adheres to fish. Food poisoning caused by it increases from summer to fall when water temperatures rise. It likes salty water, so always wash fish in plain water even if fresh, and store at low temperature. Secondary contamination is common, so wash and disinfect your hands and equipment after handling fish.

● **Staphylococcus aureus** This bacterium lives on human and animal skin and mucus, such as in wounds. It can occur in a wide variety of foods: bread and other processed grain products, fish paste products, processed meat products, etc. Prevent it from increasing and spreading by washing your hands frequently, keeping food cool, and washing and disinfecting your equipment.

● **Norovirus** Especially prevalent in winter. It is found in the vomit and feces of humans, which get flushed into the sea, where it can accumulate in shellfish; if eaten raw, or if food is contaminated by being handled by someone with the norovirus, food poisoning can occur. Wash your hands before cooking, especially after going to the bathroom.

● **E. Coli** Found in human and animal feces. Food products directly exposed to such feces become infected. Avoid by heating meat products properly, and keeping hands and equipment clean.

● **Campylobacter** Found mostly in raw or undercooked poultry. Make sure poultry is handled and cooked properly.

● **Salmonella** Mainly spread by infected eggs and meat. Raw eggs that are broken and then left for a while are susceptible to contamination. Homemade mayonnaise can cause food poisoning.

Rules for Handling Fish and Seafood

Take care to avoid contamination

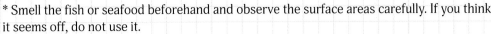

* Smell the fish or seafood beforehand and observe the surface areas carefully. If you think it seems off, do not use it.
* If sushi made with fish or seafood is not consumed on the spot and is brought home or delivered, make sure it is handled and stored at proper temperatures.

Bad practice	Good practice
Handling fish that has just been caught .	Always wash fish under running water before breaking it down. Remove the scales and organs and rinse well, then store in the refrigerator.

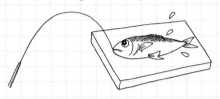

* Freshly caught fish are often covered with vibrio parahaemolyticus bacteria (see facing page).

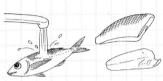

* Vibrio parahaemolyticus does not survive well in plain water, so wash fish and seafood under running tap water. Bacterial growth slows down when the temperature is under 39°F (4°C), so always store fish and seafood in the refrigerator.

Prepping food on an unwashed cutting board.

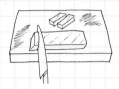

Use different cutting boards (or reverse them) for different uses.

Board for cutting fish and seafood	Board for cutting prepared food such as sushi	Board for cutting vegetables

* Use different kitchen cloths for each purpose, too.

Leaving fresh fish or seafood in its packaging until the next day.

Putting fish or seafood in an area of the refrigerator where it's frequently exposed, e.g. near the door.

Store fish and seafood in the coldest part of the refrigerator.

Or put them in airtight containers with ice packs and store in the refrigerator.

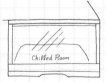

Carrying fish and seafood around for a while without refrigerating it.

Defrosting fish and seafood at room temperature.

Transport fish and seafood in insulated bags with ice packs.

Defrost fish and seafood in the refrigerator.

Touching other things with hands (or gloves) that have handled fish and seafood.*

Wash your hands (or take off your gloves) before touching other things.*

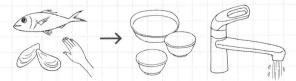

* These include phones, cameras, equipment or tools, knife handles, faucet, refrigerator door handle.

* Wash the knife handle before putting it in your hand.

PART 2

Sushi Rolls Made with Simple Shapes

This chapter includes simple decorative sushi rolls, such as flowers that celebrate the seasons, made from simple shapes and just a few basic components. These easy-to-make recipes are ideal for beginners and children.

Celebrate the Seasons

Decorative sushi is a great way to celebrate the seasons. This summer-themed presentation showcases Juicy Watermelon sushi (page 26) and Yo-yo Water Balloons sushi (page 38). A sushi mat with black strings is used to resemble the bamboo screens used by summer-festival stalls in Japan, and a fan does double duty as a placemat.

Juicy Watermelon

Difficulty level ▸ ★ **Makes 4 pieces**

This pretty watermelon shaped sushi is sure to be a hit in a bento lunchbox. Take care to scatter the black sesame seeds so that they don't overlap—they'll look just like watermelon seeds!

1 cup (202 g) Basic Sushi Rice (see page 8), divided into:
Batch 1 ½ cup (150 g)
Batch 2 scant 2 Tbsps (27 g)
Batch 3 scant 2 Tbsps (25 g)

For pink sushi rice
Mix:
   Batch 1 rice
   2 Tbsp (30 g) mentaiko

For dark green sushi rice
Mix:
   Batch 2 rice
   A little finely chopped
      nozawana-zuke pickle

For light green sushi rice
Mix:
   Batch 3 rice
   A little finely chopped
      nozawana-zuke pickle (stems only)

Additional Ingredients
A few black sesame seeds

Assembly

4 in (10 cm)

2 in (5 cm)

1 Line the sushi mat with cling film and spread the dark green sushi rice on it in a 2 x 4 in (5 x 10 cm) rectangle as shown.

2 Spread the light green sushi rice on top.

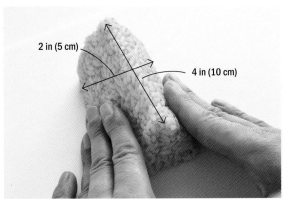

3 On a cutting board, form the pink sushi rice into a triangular shape 2 in (5 cm) wide and 4 in (10 cm) high.

2 in (5 cm)

4 in (10 cm)

4 Place the pink sushi rice on top of the Step 2 rice.

5 Pull cling film over the rice, then use the sushi mat to form it into an evenly shaped triangle.

6 Cut a little off both ends with the cling film still on to make them even, then cut the remaining sushi into 4 equal pieces.

7 Place some black sesame seeds on the surface using a toothpick, to look like watermelon seeds.

Shaved Ice Sundaes

Difficulty level ▶ ★ ★ | **Makes 4 pieces**

Shaved ice topped with sweet, colorful syrup is a summertime favorite in Japan, like a Japanese version of an ice-cream sundae. Here, I have created the look of strawberry and matcha tea ices, but you could also try mixing some finely chopped omelet to look like lemon flavor. Try coming up with your own colorful versions.

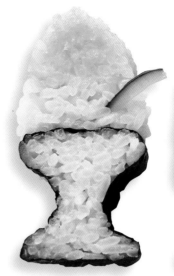

Scant 1 cup (180 g) Basic Sushi Rice (see page 8), divided into:
  Batch 1 scant ⅔ cup (130 g)
  Batch 2 2 Tbsps (25 g)
  Batch 3 2 Tbsps (25 g)

For white sushi rice
Batch 1 rice
Divide into:
  3 Tbsps (50 g)
  2½ Tbsps (40 g)
  2 x 1 Tbsp (20 g)

For pink sushi rice
Mix:
  Batch 2 rice
  ¾ tsp (5 g) oboro

For green sushi rice
Mix:
  Batch 3 rice
  ¾ tsp (5 g) green flying fish roe

Additional Ingredients
2 x 1¾ in (4.5 cm) length cucumber
  for forming the sushi
Thin strips cucumber skin for spoons

Nori piece

Half sheet

Parts

Ice (make pink and green ice with one roll) Pink sushi rice; Green sushi rice; 3 Tbsps (50 g) white sushi rice

2 portions shaved ice

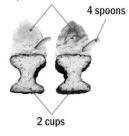

4 spoons

2 cups

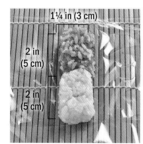

1¼ in (3 cm)
2 in (5 cm)
2 in (5 cm)

1 Line the sushi mat with cling film and place both the pink and the green sushi rice in the center so that they are each 1¼ in (3 cm) wide and 2 in (5 cm) long each as shown.

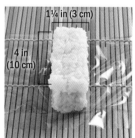

1¼ in (3 cm)
4 in (10 cm)

2 Evenly layer the white sushi rice on top of the green and pink rice. Cover with the cling film.

Sundae Glasses Half sheet nori; 2½ Tbsps (40 g) white sushi rice; 2 x 1 Tbsp (20 g) white sushi rice

1¼ in (3 cm)
4 in (10 cm)

1 Put the nori on the sushi mat and spread 1 Tbsp (20 g) white sushi rice in the middle so that it is 1¼ in (3 cm) wide.

⅔ in (1.5 cm)

2 Put the other 1 Tbsp (20 g) portion of white sushi rice on top so that it is half the width of the bottom layer.

3 Press the nori on both sides of the sushi rice, following the contours.

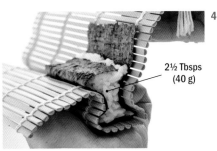

4 Holding the sushi mat in your hand, top the roll with the 2½ Tbsp (40 g) portion of white sushi rice, then wrap the nori around it so that the roll is in the shape of the sundae glass.

2½ Tbsps (40 g)

5 Press lightly to make a neat, even sundae-glass shape.

Assemble upside down.

Assembly

1 Open the cling film around the ice part and place on the sushi mat. Stack the container part on top.

sundae glass part

pink ice part

green ice part

2 Rewrap the ice part with the cling film. Put two cucumber sticks (here I've used sticks of cheese kamaboko) on each side of the container part and wrap the whole with the sushi mat. Press lightly on the cucumber to make the sundae glass shape even. Press on the ice part to make it an even triangle.

4 Add spoons made from thin strips of cucumber skin.

3 Unwrap and cut the roll to make 2 pink and 2 green ice slices.

Hibiscus Blossoms

Difficulty level ▶ ★ ★ ┃ **Makes 5 petals** ┃

Make the rice quite red so that the hibiscus flower is colorful and showy. Curving the sides of the petals gently makes the flower look more realistic.

⅔ cup (130 g) Basic Sushi Rice (see page 8), divided into:
 Batch 1 ½ cup (120 g)
 Batch 2 1 tsp (10 g)

For red sushi rice
Mix:
 Batch 1 rice
 2 Tbsps (30 g) mentaiko

For white sushi rice
1 tsp (10 g) basic sushi rice

Additional Ingredients
3 green shiso leaves
1 tsp (10 g) mentaiko
A little finely chopped Rolled Omelet (see page 19)
2 in (5 cm) pickled yamagobo or pickled carrot
 (see page 21)

Nori piece

Half sheet

Parts

Petals   Red sushi rice; Half sheet nori; White sushi rice

3 leaves

flower center

5 petals

Assembly

2 in (5 cm)

1 Place the red sushi rice in the center of the nori in a 2 in (5 cm) wide triangular shape.

⅜ in (1 cm)

2 Press down the peak of the triangle lightly to flatten it and put on the white sushi rice in a pointed triangular shape.

3 Press both sides of the triangle to make them curve slightly.

4 Place the sushi mat on your hand and wrap the nori around the rice. Press lightly to make the sides curve as shown.

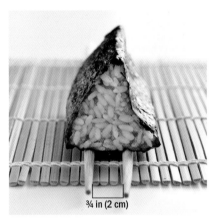

¾ in (2 cm)

5 Place 2 long cooking chopsticks on the sushi mat and put the roll on top.

6 Press the sushi mat lightly to make indentations in the roll with the chopsticks.

7 Remove the chopsticks and tidy up the sides of the roll. Cut a little off one end otherwise one petal will face the wrong way, and cut the rest into 5 even slices.

8 Place the 3 shiso leaves on a plate and the sushi petals in a flower shape. Spread a little mentaiko on the surface of each flower petal. Put a little rolled omelet on the end of the pickled yamagobo piece and insert in the middle of the petals.

Chrysanthemum Blossoms

Difficulty level ▶ ★ ★   **Makes 5 pieces**

This flower roll isn't just pretty—it smells good too, thanks to the simmered deep-fried tofu. Take care to arrange the flower petals in a nice even pattern.

For yellow sushi rice

Mix and divide into 8 equal portions:

Scant ½ cup (80 g) Basic Sushi Rice (see page 8)
2½ Tbsps (40 g) mashed Rolled Omelet (see page 19)
1 tsp toasted sesame seeds

Additional Ingredients

4 in (10 cm) length pickled yamagobo or pickled carrot
  (see page 21)
2 deep-fried tofu pockets

Nori pieces

¼ of half sheet · Half sheet · ¼ of half sheet

Parts

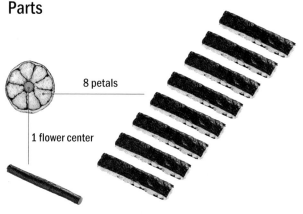

8 petals

1 flower center

Petals

8 yellow sushi rice portions; 8 x ¼ half-sheets nori

1 Put a portion of yellow sushi rice in the center of a nori piece in a thin sausage shape.

2 Place the sushi mat on your hand, fold in half and form the roll into a teardrop shape.

3 Use a square disposable chopstick to lightly press down on the middle to tidy the shape. Make 8 rolls.

Flower Center

¼ half-sheet nori; 4 in (10 cm) length pickled yamagobo

Wrap the pickled yamagobo in the nori.

Assembly

1 Place the sushi mat on your hand and, one by one, place the flower petal rolls on it to form a flower shape.

2 After 4 petal rolls have been placed, put the flower center on top.

3 Put the 4 other petal rolls on top. Press lightly as you form the flower.

4 Cut off the left and right sides of the tofu pockets and open to form a long piece as shown. Repeat for the other piece.

petals

flower center

5 Place the half sheet of nori on the sushi mat. Put the 2 opened tofu pockets on top of the nori and cut off any bits that protrude beyond the edges of the nori.

6 Place the assembled flower in the center of the 2 pieces of tofu. Hold the sushi mat in your hand and wrap the flower. Overlap the long edge of the nori and close the roll.

7 Transfer the closed roll to the edge of the sushi mat and tidy up the shape so that is forms a neat circle. Let the roll rest until the nori has softened a bit, then cut into 5 even slices.

Camellias

Difficulty level ▸ ★ ★ **Makes 4 pieces**

This beautiful camellia design will appeal to sushi lovers of all ages. It looks great in a party buffet spread, and also makes a beautiful gift.

1 ⅔ cups (330 g) Basic Sushi Rice (see page 8), divided into:
  Batch 1 Scant 1 cup (180 g)
  Batch 2 ¾ cup (150 g)

For red sushi rice	For white sushi rice
Batch 1 rice	Batch 2 rice
1¼ Tbsp (20 g) mentaiko	1 tsp toasted sesame seeds
1 tsp finely chopped red pickled ginger	*Mix and divide into:*
Mix and divide into:	⅓ cup (70 g)
2 x scant ½ cups (80 g)	2½ Tbsps (40 g)
3 x 1 Tbsp (15 g) portions	2 Tbsps (30 g)
	1½ tsps (10 g)

Additional Ingredients
4 in (10 cm) length of cucumber
⅔ x ⅔ x 4 in (1.5 x 1.5 x 10 cm)
  piece Rolled Omelet (see page 19)

Nori pieces

Half sheet	½ of half sheet	½ of half sheet	⅔ of half sheet	
Half sheet	⅔ of half sheet	⅓ of half sheet		

1¼ in (3 cm)

Parts

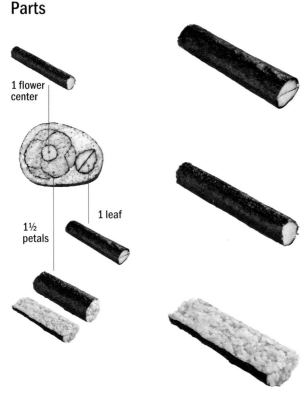

1 flower center

1 leaf

1½ petals

Leaf
4 in (10 cm) length of cucumber; 1¼ in (3 cm) wide nori piece; half sheet nori

Cut the cucumber into 3, as shown in the diagram (right). Discard the center piece. Put the 1¼ in (3 cm) nori piece between the 2 remaining cucumber pieces and wrap with the large nori piece.

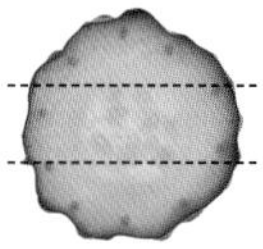

Flower Center
⅔ x ⅔ x 4 in (1.5 x 1.5 x 10 cm) piece Rolled Omelet; ⅓ half-sheet nori

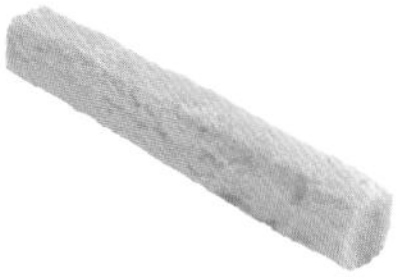

Cut the corners off the piece of omelet to make them rounded. Wrap with the nori.

Petals
2 x ⅔ half-sheets nori; 2 x scant ½ cups (80 g) red sushi rice

Place a ⅔ half-sheet of nori on the sushi mat. Put 1 portion of red sushi rice in the center of the nori and roll it into a fat sausage shape. Repeat to make 2 rolls and cut each in half. Cut 3 of the halves into half lengthwise.

Flower Petals (see facing page); Flower Center (see facing page); 3 x 1 Tbsp (15 g) portions red sushi rice; ½ half-sheet nori

1 Put 2 petal pieces around the flower center piece. Fill the 3 gaps between the petal pieces with the red sushi rice.

2 Place the ½ half-sheet of nori on the mat. Put the piece from Step 1 on the nori and form a roll.

Assembly

1 ½ tsps (10 g)

⅓ cup (70 g) · 6 in (15 cm)

1 Place 1 half sheet of nori and ½ a half-sheet of nori on the mat and connect them with a few rice grains. Spread ⅓ cup (70 g) white sushi rice in the middle 6 in (15 cm) wide. Form 1½ tsps (10 g) white sushi rice into a triangle and place on top, slightly to the right of center.

2 Place the flower roll on the left of the triangular sushi rice and the Leaf (see facing page) on the right.

3 Fill the gap between the flower roll and the leaf with 2½ Tbsps (40 g) white sushi rice.

Stack up in order.

flower

leaf

flower center

2½ Tbsps (40 g)

2 Tbsps (30 g)

4 Put the sushi mat on your hand and evenly cover the top of the nori roll with 2 Tbsps (30 g) white sushi rice. Close the roll while squeezing it from the sides and bottom.

5 Transfer the roll to the edge of the sushi mat. Tidy the ends, and cut the roll into 4 even slices.

PART 3

Animal-shaped Sushi Rolls

These cute animal sushi rolls have great visual impact and are sure to be a hit whether at picnics, parties or in lunchboxes. Have fun experimenting with different facial expressions by varying the size and position of the eyes.

Cute Sushi for Picnics or Parties!

Cute Shiba-inu the Dog sushi rolls (page 44) and Paw Prints sushi rolls (page 46) are a fun and eyecatching addition to a kids' party or picnic. If you wrap the sushi slices individually, this makes it easy for guests to take your sushi home.

Mikeneko the Cat

Difficulty level ▶ ★ ★ | Makes 4 pieces

Tricolored cats, called mikeneko, are common in Japan. For maximum cuteness, make sure you form the face so that the forehead is narrow and the chin is wider.

1 ⅓ cups (275 g) Basic Sushi Rice (see page 8), divided into:
 Batch 1 1 cup (200 g)
 Batch 2 3 Tbsps (45 g)
 Batch 3 2 Tbsps (30 g)

For white sushi rice
Batch 1 rice
2 Tbsps (30 g) finely chopped
 bettarazuke pickles
1 tsp toasted white sesame seeds
Mix and divide into:
 ¼ cup (60 g)
 2 x 2 Tbsps (30 g)
 4 x 1 Tbsp (20 g)
 3 x 1½ tsps (10 g)

For black sushi rice
Batch 2 rice
1 tsp ground black sesame seeds
Mix and divide into:
 1 heaping Tbsp (20 g)
 1 Tbsp (15 g)
 1½ tsps (10 g)

For brown sushi rice
Batch 3 rice
¾ tsp (5 g) chicken soboro (see page 20)
Mix and divide into:
 1 heaping Tbsp (20 g)
 1 Tbsp (15 g)

Additional Ingredients
4 in (10 cm) length fish sausage,
 quartered (just 1 quarter is used)
4 in (10 cm) length pickled yamagobo or
 pickled carrot (see page 21)

Nori pieces

| Half sheet | ⅓ of half sheet | ¼ of half sheet | |
| ½ of half sheet | ½ of half sheet | | 1½ in (4 cm) |

make the eyes and whiskers
with the remaining nori

Parts

2 ears

8 eyes

1 nose

16 whiskers

1 mouth

Ears 4 in (10 cm) length fish sausage, quartered lengthwise (see diagram, left); 2 x ½ half-sheets nori; 2 x 1 Tbsps (20 g) white sushi rice

Cut one of the quarters of fish sausage in half lengthwise to make 2 pieces (see diagram). Cut the other 3 quarters into strips about 2⅓–2¾ in (6–7 cm) long. Put a strip of fish sausage in the middle of one of the ½ half-sheets of nori and cover the sausage with one portion of white sushi rice. Wrap the roll into a triangular shape. Repeat to make a second roll. Cut each roll into 4 equal pieces.

Nose 1 piece yamagobo; ¼ half-sheet nori

Wrap the yamagobo piece with the nori.

Assembly

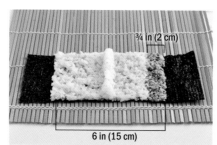

¾ in (2 cm)

6 in (15 cm)

1 Place the half sheet of nori and the ⅓ half-sheet of nori on the mat and connect them at the edges with a few rice grains. Put ¼ cup (60 g) of white sushi rice and 1½ tsps (10 g) of black sushi rice in the middle, about 6 in (15 cm) wide. The black rice should take up about ¾ in (2 cm). Place a 1½ tsp (10 g) portion of white sushi rice in the center and form into a pointed triangular shape.

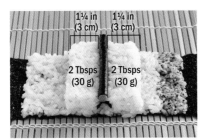

2 Fold the 1½ in (4 cm) wide nori strip in half lengthwise and stick the halves together with a few rice grains. Fold in half again and press onto the white sushi rice strip in a triangular shape, to make the mouth.

3 Place 2 Tbsp (30 g) portions of white sushi rice on both sides of the mouth so that each portion is 1¼ in (3 cm) wide. Place the nose piece in the center.

4 Place 1 Tbsp (20 g) portions of white rice on both sides of the nose.

5 Put 1½ tsps (10 g) of white sushi rice, 1 heaping Tbsp (20 g) each of brown sushi rice and black sushi rice on top, in the order shown.

Stack up in order.

1½ tsps (10 g)   1 Tbsp (20 g)   1 Tbsp (20 g)

nose

mouth

1 Tbsp (15 g)
1 Tbsp (15 g)
1½ tsps (10 g)

6 Place the sushi mat on your hand and cover the top of the roll with sushi rice in this order from left to right: 1½ tsps (10 g) white sushi rice, 1 Tbsp (15 g) brown sushi rice and 1 Tbsp (15 g) black sushi rice. Wrap the nori over the rice using the sushi mat, first one side and then the other.

7 Move the roll to the edge of the sushi mat and tidy the ends. Cut the roll into 4 equal pieces.

8 Add the ears and put on the eyes and whiskers, made with leftover nori.

Variation: An all-white cat made just with white sushi rice is very cute too.

Shiba-inu the Dog

Difficulty level ▶ ★ ★ ★ [Makes 4 pieces]

Long a favorite breed in Japan, the shiba-inu is also becoming popular overseas. To make this little pup look even more adorable, pay attention to the position of the ears, spreading them out rather than putting them too close together.

1 ⅔ cups (330 g) Basic Sushi Rice (see page 8), divided into:
  Batch 1 ¾ cup (150 g)
  Batch 2 Scant 1 cup (180 g)

For white sushi rice
Batch 1 rice
1 heaping tsp (20g) finely chopped
  sushi ginger
1 tsp toasted white sesame seeds
Mix and divide into:
  2 x 3 Tbsps (50 g)
  2 x 2 Tbsps (30 g)
  2 x ¾ tsp (5 g)

For brown sushi rice
Batch 2 rice
1 heaping Tbsp (20 g) chicken
  soboro (see page)
Mix and divide into:
  just over ¼ cup (60 g)
  3 Tbsps (50 g)
  2 x 2 Tbsps (30 g)
  1 heaping Tbsp (20 g)
  1½ tsps (10 g)

Nori pieces

Half sheet	½ of half sheet	¼ of half sheet	¼ of half sheet

½ of half sheet	½ of half sheet	⅔ of half sheet

use for the nose, mouth and eyes

Parts

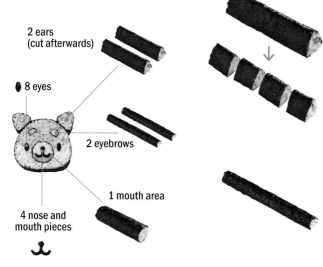

2 ears
(cut afterwards)

8 eyes

2 eyebrows

1 mouth area

4 nose and
mouth pieces

Ears 2 Tbsps brown sushi rice; 2 x ½ half-sheet nori

Place 2 Tbsps brown sushi rice on one edge of one ½ half-sheet nori in a thin sausage shape and roll to form a triangle. Repeat to make 2. Cut each into 4 equal slices to make 8 ear pieces.

Eyebrows 2 x ¾ tsp (5 g) portions white sushi rice; 2 x ¼ half-sheets nori

Place ¾ tsp sushi rice in the middle of one of the ¼ half-sheets of nori in a thin sausage. Roll and press down lightly to form an oval shape. Repeat to make 2.

Mouth Area

3 Tbsps (50 g) white rice; ⅔ half-sheet nori

Place the rice in the middle of the nori in a sausage shape. Roll to form a round roll.

Nose, Mouth and Eyes

Cut out the shapes as shown, using the leftover piece of nori.

Assembly

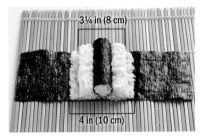

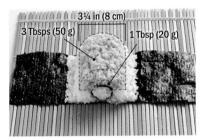

1 Place the half sheet of nori and a ½ half-sheet of nori on the mat and connect them at the edges with a few rice grains. Place 3 Tbsps (50 g) white sushi rice in the center, spreading to 4 in (10 cm) wide. Place the mouth area piece on top in the center. Put a 2 Tbsp (30 g) portion of white sushi rice on both sides of the mouth area roll to support it and fill in the gaps.

2 Put 1 heaping Tbsp (20 g) brown sushi rice on top of the mouth area piece, covering the nori. Top this with another 3 Tbsps (50 g) of brown sushi rice in a dome shape. The brown sushi rice should be about 3 in (8 cm) wide.

3 Place a 1½ tsp (10 g) strip of brown sushi rice on top of the domed rice so that it is ⅔ in (1.5 cm) wide, and place the two eyebrow rolls on both sides.

4 Place just over ¼ cup (60 g) brown sushi rice on top in a half-moon shape as shown.

eyebrow

mouth area

Stack up in order.

5 Place the sushi mat on your hand and close the roll so that it forms a gently curved triangular shape with the bottom part wider than the top.

6 Tidy the ends and cut into 4 equal slices.

7 Add the ears and finish by putting on the eyes and nose and mouth nori parts.

Cheeky Monkeys

Difficulty level ▶ ★ ★ ★   **Makes 4 pieces**

With ears made from wrapping sushi rice around sticks of cheese, these cheeky monkey rolls are as tasty as they are cute!

1½ cups (310 g) Basic Sushi Rice (see page 8), divided into:
- **Batch 1** ¾ cup (150 g)
- **Batch 2** ¾ cup (160 g)

For white sushi rice
Batch 1 rice
A little finely chopped sushi ginger
1 tsp white sesame seeds
Mix and divide into:
- 3 Tbsps (50 g)
- 2½ Tbsps (40 g)
- 2 x 1 Tbsp (20 g)
- 3 x 1½ tsps (10 g)

For brown sushi rice
Batch 2 rice
2 Tbsps (30 g) chicken soboro (see page 20)
Mix and divide into:
- Scant ½ cup (80 g)
- 2 x 2 Tbsps (30 g)
- 2 x 2 scant Tbsps (25 g)

Additional Ingredients
4 in (10 cm) length pickled yamagobo or pickled carrot (see page 21)
4 in (10 cm) length cheese kamaboko

Nori pieces

Half sheet	¼ of half sheet			⅓ of half sheet

Half sheet	½ of half sheet	½ of half sheet

use for the eyes

Parts

2 ears (cut afterwards)

8 eyes

1 nose piece

1 mouth piece

Ears
1 cheese kamaboko; 2 x ¼ half-sheets nori;
2 x ½ half-sheets nori; 2 x 2 scant Tbsps (25 g) brown sushi rice

1. Slice the cheese kamaboko in half lengthwise.

2. Wrap each cheese kamaboko half in a ¼ half-sheet of nori. Place one half cut side down in the center of a ½ half-sheet of nori. Cover with 1 scant Tbsp (25 g) of brown sushi rice as shown.

3. Make 2 pieces, then cut each piece into 4 equal lengths to make a total of 8 ear pieces.

Mouth
1 x ¼ half-sheet nori; 1½ tsp (10 g) portion white sushi rice

1. Place the nori on the sushi mat horizontally and wrap the sushi rice.

2. Secure the roll with a few rice grains used as glue.

3. Cut the roll in half lengthwise.

Nose
¼ half-sheet nori; yamagobo

Wrap the yamagobo in the nori.

Eyes
Leftover nori

Cut out the eyes from the nori.

Face Half sheet nori; white sushi rice: 3 Tbsps (50g) ; 1½ tsps (10g); 2½ Tbsps (40g); 2 x 1 Tbsp (20g)

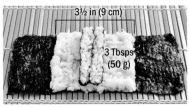

1 Place the sushi mat sideways. Put a half sheet of nori on top horizontally. Spread 3 Tbsps (50 g) white sushi rice in the middle, 3½ in (9 cm) wide. Place the mouth parts (2 halves) in the center.

2 Put 1½ tsps (10 g) white sushi rice on both sides of the mouth pieces so that they are the same height as the mouth pieces. Put the nose piece on top in the center.

3 Place 2½ Tbsps (40 g) white sushi rice on top and wrap it around the nose and mouth pieces.

4 Place the sushi mat on your hand. Squeeze the mat from both sides to round the roll and place 2 x 1 Tbsp (20 g) white sushi rice portions formed into sausages on top. Make each edge stick out a bit from the sushi mat.

5 Wrap the sushi mat around following the contour of the indent, and close the roll while pressing the mat. Press so that the part of the face where the eyes will go is indented a little on both sides. Tidy the shape.

Assembly

1 To make the head, connect a half sheet of nori and the ⅓ half-sheet nori together with rice grains on the edges, and place on the horizontal sushi mat. Place the face piece in the middle and put a 2 Tbsp (30 g) portion of brown sushi rice on either side to support the face. Make the rice about the same height as the face piece.

head

eye positions

scant ½ cup (80 g)

Stack up in order.

2 Top with a scant ½ cup (80 g) brown sushi rice and wrap in a rounded shape.

nose   mouth

3 Place the sushi mat on your hand and close the roll.

4 Shift the roll to the edge of the sushi mat and tidy the ends.

5 Cut into 4 equal slices, then add the eyes and ears to each head.

Playful Sea Lions

Difficulty level ▶ ★ ★ ★ `Makes 4 pieces`

This striking green and black sushi roll shows
a sea lion playing with a ball. Make sure the
sea lion's chest doesn't curve out too much.

1½ cups (300 g) Basic Sushi Rice (see page 8), divided into:
Batch 1 ¾ cup (150 g)
Batch 2 ¾ cup (150 g)

For green sushi rice
Batch 1 rice
1½ tsps (10 g) green flying fish roe
1 Tbsp (20 g) finely chopped
   nozawana-zuke pickles
   (stems and leaves)
Mix and divide into:
   Scant ½ cup (80 g)
   ¼ cup (60 g)
   2 Tbsps (30 g)
   1½ tsps (10 g)

For black sushi rice
Batch 2 rice
1 Tbsp ground black sesame seeds
1 tsp yukari powder
Mix and divide into:
   ½ cup (100 g)
   3 Tbsps (50 g)

Additional Ingredients
4 in (10 cm) length cheese kamaboko
A little crab stick

Nori pieces

Half sheet	Half sheet

½ of half sheet		⅔ of half sheet	⅓ of half sheet

use for the eyes

Parts

Ball cheese kamaboko; ⅓ half-sheet nori

Wrap the cheese with the nori piece.

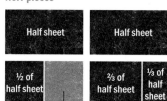

1 ball

4 eyes

1 body

Body 1 half sheet nori; ⅔ half-sheet nori; 3 Tbsps (50 g) black sushi rice;
1½ tsps (10 g) green sushi rice; ½ cup (100 g) black sushi rice

4 in (10 cm)

1 Line the sushi mat with
cling film. Place the two nori
pieces on the cling film and
connect them at the edges
with a few rice grains. Spread
the 3 Tbsps (50 g) of black
sushi rice in the middle so
that it is 4 in (10 cm) wide.

When the rice and nori have been folded,
press lightly so that the folds lay flat.

⅜ in (1 cm)

¾ in (2 cm) ¾ in (2 cm)

2 in (5 cm)

1½ tsp (10 g)

2 Turn the whole
thing over so that
the nori is on top.
Fold the rice and
nori inwards on
both sides, leaving
a ⅜ in (1 cm) gap
in the middle (see
diagram above).

3 Place the 1½ tsps (10 g)
of green sushi rice in the
indent.

4 Turn over the assembled part from Step 3 and place the ½ cup (100 g) of black sushi rice on top in a triangular shape so that the point of the triangle is a slightly to the left of center of the bottom piece.

5 Make an indent on the right side with your finger while supporting the rice with your left hand, to form the neck. Wrap the nori around the rice following its contours.

6 Form the shape of a sea lion using the sushi mat. Press firmly to make the shape stable.

Assembly

1 Place a half sheet of nori and a ½ half-sheet of nori on the mat and connect them at the edges with a few rice grains. Place the body part in the center. Put the ¼ cup (60 g) of green sushi rice on the left and the scant ½ cup (80 g) green sushi rice on the right of the body part.

2 Place the ball part on top of the body part, in between the sushi rice.

3 Place 2 Tbsps (30 g) green sushi rice in a dome over the ball part and down the sides and roll.

Stack up in order.

body

2 Tbsps (30 g)

ball

4 Shift the roll to the edge of the sushi mat and tidy the ends. Cut into 4 even pieces. Decorate the ball with the crab stick pieces and add the eyes to finish.

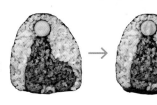

PART 4

Assorted Shapes

If you've mastered the sushi rolls in Parts 2 and 3 of this book, why not challenge yourself with the assorted shapes in this chapter? From Pretty Bows to Cute Helicopters, you're sure to impress your friends and family!

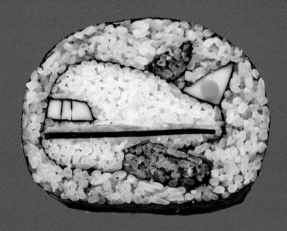

Stunning Sushi, Simply Served

If you're making sushi pieces with lots of different colors and components like these Beautiful Autumn Sky Rolls (page 60), it's best to serve them on a simple white plate, with a plain or light-colored tablecloth. The low-key background elements will serve to enhance the stunning details of your creation.

Pretty Bows

This is a square sushi roll with a pretty bow in the middle. Build up both sides alternately to achieve a well-balanced result.

1 ⅔ cups (340 g) Basic Sushi Rice (see page 8), divided into:
  Batch 1 1 cup (200 g)
  Batch 2 ⅔ cup (140 g)

For pink sushi rice
Batch 1 rice
2½ Tbsps (40 g) oboro
Mix and divide into:
  2 x 2 heaping Tbsps (35 g)
  2 x 2 Tbsps (30 g)
  5 x 1 Tbsp (20 g)
  2 x ¾ tsp (5 g)

For yellow sushi rice
Batch 2 rice
1 heaping Tbsp (20 g) finely chopped
  Rolled Omelet (see page 19)
1 Tbsp (15 g) finely chopped yellow
  takuan pickles
Mix and divide into:
  Scant ½ cup (80 g)
  2 x 2 Tbsps (25 g)
  1 Tbsp (15 g)
  2 x 1½ tsp (10 g)
  2 x 1 tsp (5 g)

Nori pieces

| Half sheet | ⅔ of half sheet | ⅓ of half sheet | ⅔ of half sheet | |
| ½ of half sheet | ½ of half sheet | ⅔ of half sheet | | |

1¼ in (3 cm) x 2

Parts

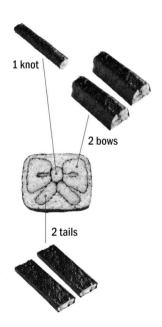

1 knot

2 bows

2 tails

Knot   ⅓ half-sheet nori; 1 Tbsp (20 g) pink sushi rice

Form the sushi rice into a thin sausage and place in the middle of the nori. Form into an oval roll.

Bows   2 x ⅔ half-sheets nori; 2 x 1¼ in (3 cm) wide nori pieces;
2 x ¾ tsp (5 g) portions pink sushi rice; 2 x 2 heaping Tbsps (35 g)
portions pink sushi rice; 4 x 1 Tbsp (20 g) portions pink sushi rice

¼ in (5 mm)

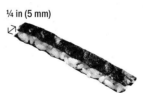

1½ in (4 cm)

2 Tbsps (35 g)

1 Spread ¾ tsp (5 g) pink sushi rice on half a 1¼ in (3 cm) wide nori piece.

2 Fold in half, leaving ¼ in (5 mm) on the edge as shown.

3 Spread 2 heaping Tbsps (35 g) of pink sushi rice on a ⅔ half-sheet of nori so that it is about 1½ in (4 cm) wide.

4 Put the Step 2 piece in the center of the Step 3 piece with the folded edge facing down. Put 1 Tbsp (20 g) portions of pink sushi rice on both sides to support it. Form the rice into a trapezoid shape as you wrap the nori around.

¾ in (2 cm)

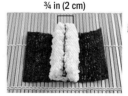

Make 2 pieces.

1¼ in (3 cm)   ¾ in (2 cm)

Tails   2 x ½ half-sheets nori
2 x heaping Tbsps (30 g) portions pink sushi rice
2 x ¾ tsp (5 g) portions yellow sushi rice

1 For each piece, wrap 2 heaping Tbsps (30 g) of pink rice in the nori and form into a thin rectangle.

2 Spread the yellow sushi rice on top so that it is about ¾ in (2 cm) wide.

Assembly

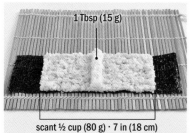

1 Place the half sheet of nori and a ⅔ half-sheet of nori horizontally on the mat and connect them at the edges with a few rice grains. Spread a scant ½ cup (80 g) of yellow sushi rice in the middle, 7 in (18 cm) wide. Place 1 Tbsp (15 g) of yellow sushi rice in a strip down the center.

1 Tbsp (15 g)

scant ½ cup (80 g) · 7 in (18 cm)

2 Place the knot piece on the strip, then the bow pieces on each side. Place the tail pieces on the bow pieces so that the yellow sushi rice sides are against the bow pieces, and the nori sides are facing the center.

1½ tsps (10 g)

2 Tbsps (25 g)

1½ tsps (10 g)

Assemble upside down.

tail

bow

knot

3 Place a 1½ tsp (10 g) portion of yellow sushi rice on the outer sides of the tails and 2 Tbsps (25 g) of yellow sushi rice in the middle.

4 Place the sushi mat on your hand and top the roll with 2 Tbsps (25 g) yellow sushi rice. Close the roll and form into a square shape.

5 Shift the roll to the edge of the sushi mat and tidy the ends. Cut into 4 equal slices.

Beautiful Autumn Sky Rolls

Difficulty level ▶ ★ ★　[**Makes 4 pieces**]

The graduated colors in this decorative sushi roll are very pretty. It takes a little time to make the different colored sushi rice, but this recipe isn't difficult, even for beginners.

1 ⅓ cups (270 g) Basic Sushi Rice (see page 8), divided into:
Batch 1 ½ cup (90 g)	**Batch 4** 2 Tbsps (30 g)
Batch 2 ¼ cup (55 g)	**Batch 5** 2 Tbsps (25 g)
Batch 3 ¼ cup (55 g)	**Batch 6** 1 Tbsp (15 g)

For green-black sushi rice
Batch 1 rice
1½ tsps (10 g) finely chopped
　nozawana-zuke pickles
1 tsp ground black sesame seeds
Mix and divide into:
　¼ cup (60 g)
　2½ Tbsps (40 g)

For purple-black sushi rice
Mix:
　Batch 2 rice
　1 tsp yukari powder
　1 tsp ground black sesame seeds

For pink sushi rice
Mix:
　Batch 3 rice
　¾ tsp (5 g) oboro

For orange-pink sushi rice
Mix:
　Batch 4 rice
　¾ tsp (5 g) oboro
　¾ tsp (5 g) orange flying fish roe

For yellow sushi rice
Mix:
　Batch 5 rice
　¾ tsp (5 g) finely chopped Rolled Omelet
　　(see page 19)

For orange sushi rice
Mix:
　Batch 6 rice
　¾ tsp (5 g) orange flying fish roe

Additional Ingredients
4 in (10 cm) length cheese kamaboko

Nori pieces

| Half sheet | ½ of half sheet | ⅓ of half sheet |
| Half sheet | | use for dragonflies |

Parts

- ● 16 eyes
- ▬ 32 wings
- ▬ 8 bodies
- 1 sun
- 1 mountain

Sun　⅓ half-sheet nori; 4 in (10 cm) length cheese kamaboko

Cut off one side of the cheese kamaboko lengthwise to make it flat. Wrap with the nori.

Mountain　1 half sheet nori; ¼ cup (60 g) green-black sushi rice; 2½ Tbsps (40 g) portion green-black sushi rice

¼ cup (60 g)

2½ Tbsps (40 g) · 2⅓ in (6 cm)

Place the nori on the sushi mat. Put the 2½ Tbsp (40 g) portion of green-black sushi rice in the center and spread it 2⅓ in (6 cm) wide. Put the ¼ cup (60 g) portion of green-black sushi rice on top and form into a mountain shape, higher on the right side. Wrap the nori round the rice to make a wedge shaped roll.

Assembly

1 Place 1 half sheet of nori and a ½ half-sheet of nori horizontally on the sushi mat and connect them at the edges with a few rice grains. Place the mountain piece a little to the right of center on the nori and place the sun piece on the flat part of the mountain with the flat side down.

2 Spread the yellow sushi rice over sun and mountain, following the contours.

3 Spread the pink sushi rice over the yellow rice, followed by the orange-pink sushi rice and the orange sushi rice.

4 Finish with the purple-black sushi rice. Square off the top and wrap the nori around to form the roll.

Stack up in order.

sun

mountain

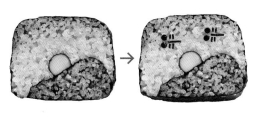

5 Shift the roll to the edge of the sushi mat and tidy the ends. Cut into 4 equal slices.

6 Top with dragonflies cut out of nori.

Cheers! Party Rolls

Difficulty level ▶ ★ ★ ★ ★　`Makes 4 pieces`

When the roll is cut and the slices flipped and placed with the beer steins facing each other, it looks like two people making a toast!

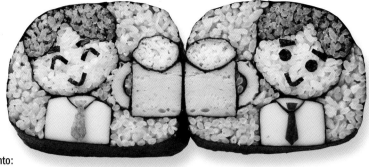

1 cup + 2 Tbsps (230 g) Basic Sushi Rice (see page 8), divided into:
- **Batch 1** ½ cup (110 g)
- **Batch 2** ⅓ cup (70 g)
- **Batch 3** 3 Tbsps (50 g)

For red sushi rice
Batch 1 rice
1 Tbsp (15 g) mentaiko
½ tsp white sesame seeds
Mix and divide into:
- 2½ Tbsps (40 g)
- 2 x 2 Tbsps (30 g)
- 1 Tbsp (15 g);
- 2 x ¾ tsp (5 g)

For white sushi rice
Batch 2 rice

For black sushi rice
Mix:
- Batch 3 rice
- 1 Tbsp ground black sesame seeds
- ½ tsp yukari powder

Additional ingredients
1 white kamaboko fish cake
4 in (10 cm) length chikuwa, halved lengthwise
1 x ¾ x 4 in (2.5 x 2 x 10 cm) piece Rolled Omelet (see page 19)
3 crab sticks
a little cucumber

Nori pieces

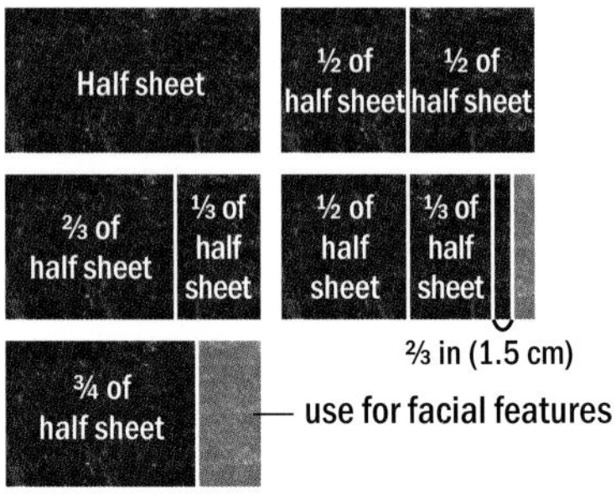

Half sheet	½ of half sheet	½ of half sheet
⅔ of half sheet	⅓ of half sheet	½ of half sheet	⅓ of half sheet
¾ of half sheet		⅔ in (1.5 cm)

— use for facial features

Parts

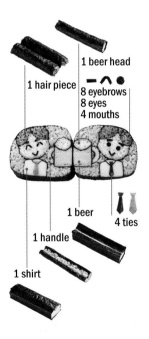

1 beer head

1 hair piece

8 eyebrows
8 eyes
4 mouths

1 beer

1 handle

1 shirt

4 ties

Beer　½ half-sheet nori; 1 x ¾ x 4 in (2.5 x 2 x 10 cm) piece Rolled Omelet

Cut out the middle of the omelet as shown. Wrap in the nori. It is OK if the nori does not go all the way around the cut out part since this will be covered by the beer foam.

5 in (2 cm)
4 in (10 cm)
1 in (2.5 cm)

Beer Foam　⅓ half-sheet nori; 3 crab sticks

Take the red part off the crab sticks and reserve. Shred the white part, then reassemble into a stick the same length as the nori. Wrap in the nori.

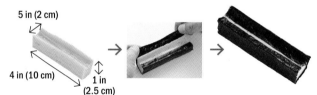

Shirt　⅔ half-sheet nori; ⅔ in (1.5 cm) wide nori piece; 1 kamaboko

Cut off both sides of the kamaboko to leave a 1¼ in (3 cm) wide piece. Cut out a V-shaped piece from the top. Place the ⅔ in (1.5 cm) wide nori piece in the indentation and put the cut out piece back. Put the kamaboko in the center of the ⅔ nori piece and wrap.

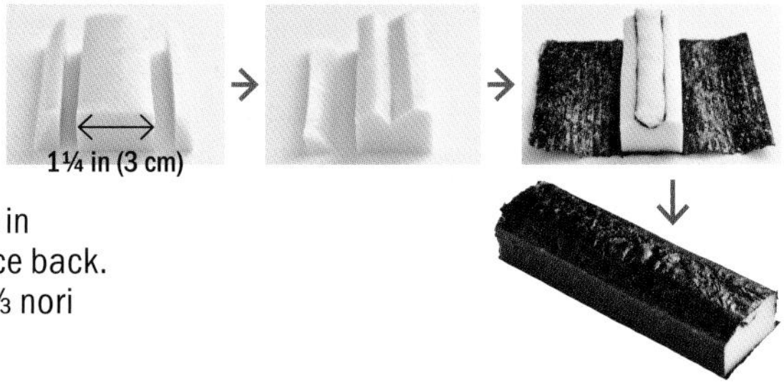

1¼ in (3 cm)

Handle　⅓ half-sheet nori; ¾ tsp (5 g) red sushi rice; 4 in (10 cm) length chikuwa halved lengthwise

Wrap the chikuwa with the nori. Put the red sushi rice in the middle of the chikuwa, making sure it does not extend beyond the ends.

Hair ½ half-sheet nori; all the black sushi rice

Place the nori on the sushi mat and put the sushi rice formed into a rectangle in the center. Roll and cut into half lengthwise.

Face ¾ half-sheet nori; all the white sushi rice; hair pieces

Place the nori piece on the sushi mat and put the 2 hair piece halves in the center with the cut sides down. Take a little of the white sushi rice and stuff it between the hair pieces. Top with the rest of the sushi rice and form into a rectangle. Wrap the nori around it to form a roll.

Assembly

2 Tbsps (30 g)

1¼ in (3 cm)

1 Put the half sheet of nori and a ½ half-sheet of nori horizontally on the mat and connect them at the edges with a few rice grains. Put the shirt piece and 2 Tbsps (30 g) red sushi rice formed into a 1¼ in (3 cm) wide strip side by side in the center of the nori. Place the beer and foam on the left side of the red sushi rice strip.

¾ tsp (5 g)

2 Place the handle next to the beer and stuff the gap between that and the shirt with ¾ tsp (5 g) red sushi rice.

3 Place the face roll on top of the shirt at a slight angle, and put 2½ Tbsps (40 g) red sushi rice on the side of the shirt to support the head. Stuff 1 Tbsp (15 g) red sushi rice in the gap between the head and the beer stein handle and top with 2 Tbsps (30 g) red sushi rice. Place the sushi mat on your hand and close up the roll.

Stack up in order.

face

2 Tbsps (30 g)

2½ Tbsps (40 g)

handle

¾ tsp (15 g)

beer foam

beer

shirt

4 Shift the roll to the edge of the sushi mat and tidy the ends. Cut into 4 equal slices.

5 Add eyebrows, eyes and mouths cut out of nori. Make tiny neckties with the red part of the crab sticks used for the beer foam and strips of cucumber and place on the slices.

Airplane Rolls

Difficulty level ▶ ★ ★ ★ ★ ★ **Makes 4 pieces**

This delightful, rounded airplane is perfect for going away parties, or to liven up any kid's birthday celebration.

Scant 2 cups (380 g) Basic Sushi Rice (see page 8), divided into:
Batch 1 1 cup (200 g)
Batch 2 ⅔ cup (140 g)
Batch 3 2½ Tbsps (40 g)

For green sushi rice
Batch 1 rice
1 Tbsp (20 g) green flying fish roe
Mix and divide into:
½ cup (100 g)
2½ Tbsps (40 g)
2 x 1 heaping Tbsp (20 g)
2 x 1 Tbsp (15 g)
1½ tsps (10 g)

For white sushi rice
Batch 2 sushi rice
1 tsp toasted white sesame seeds
Mix and divide into:
⅓ cup (70 g)
2½ Tbsps (40 g)
2 Tbsps (30 g)

For purple sushi rice
Batch 3 rice
1 teaspoon yukari powder
Mix and divide into:
1½ tsps (10 g)
2 Tbsps (30 g)

Additional Ingredients
4 in (10 cm) length kamaboko fish cake
1 crab stick
A little pickled yamagobo or pickled carrot (see page 21)

Nori pieces

Half sheet		Half sheet	
⅔ of half sheet	⅓ of half sheet	½ of half sheet	⅓ of half sheet
⅓ of half sheet	2 x ¼ in (5 mm)		

Parts

2 small wings
1 tail
1 plane body
4 decorations
2 large wings

Cutting the Kamaboko

4 in (10 cm)
¾ in (2 cm)
1 in (2.5 cm)

1 Cut a ¾ x 1 x 4 in (2 x 2.5 x 10 cm) piece from the curved side of the kamaboko.

⅔ in (1.5 cm)
¼ in (5 mm)
¼ in (5 mm)

2 Cut the block into 3 strips 1 x ⅔ in (1.5 cm) wide and 2 x ¼ in (5 mm) wide.

A Lay the middle piece on its side and cut into 3 pieces as shown (for the windows).

B Cut the largest piece diagonally (for the tail).

Tail   ⅓ half-sheet nori; kamaboko B above
Put the kamaboko B part on the nori and wrap.

Large Wing   ½ half-sheet nori; 2 Tbsps (30 g) purple sushi rice

1¾ in (4 cm)

Put the nori on the sushi mat, place the sushi rice in the center and spread it 1¾ in (4 cm) wide. Make the near side thicker and the far side thinner. Wrap the nori around the rice and form into a wing shape.

Small Wing   ⅓ half-sheet nori; 1½ tsps (10 g) purple sushi rice
Put the nori on the sushi mat. Place the sushi rice in the center in a sausage shape and form a triangular roll.

Body 2 x ¼ in (5 mm) nori pieces; kamaboko A pieces (facing page); ⅓ half-sheet nori; 1 half sheet nori. White sushi rice: ⅓ cup (70 g) ; 2 Tbsps (30 g); 2½ Tbsps (40 g). Green sushi rice: 1 Tbsp (15 g); 2 x 1 heaping Tbsp (20 g); 1½ tsps (10 g)

2 Tbsps (30 g)   2½ Tbsps (40 g)

direction of the windows

⅓ cup (70 g) · 2¾ in (7 cm)

1 Put the ¼ in (5 mm) nori pieces between the kamaboko A pieces. Wrap with the ⅓ half-sheet of nori to make the windows.

2 Put the half sheet of nori on the mat. Spread ⅓ cup (70 g) white rice on the center, 2¾ in (7 cm) wide, slanting on the right. Place the Step 1 windows on the left, pointing right. Put 2 Tbsps (30 g) white rice on the windows and 2½ Tbsps (40 g) white rice to its right, slanting to the right. Fill in any gaps. Curve the rice gently. Wrap the nori around it.

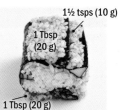

1 Tbsp (15 g)

1½ tsps (10 g)

1 Tbsp (20 g)

1 Tbsp (20 g)

3 Turn the roll over and make a cut in the top. Make a groove for inserting the large wing piece.

4 Place the sushi mat on your hand. Insert the wide end of the large wing piece into the groove.

5 Put 1 Tbsp (15 g) green sushi rice under the large wing piece and 1 heaping Tbsp (20 g) green sushi rice on the window side of the large wing piece.

6 Turn the roll over so the large wing piece is on the bottom. Place on the cutting board. Put on the small wing piece and tail wing piece and put on 1½ tsps (10 g) and 2 × heaping Tbsps (20 g) of green sushi rice as shown.

Assembly

large wing

small wing

Stack up in order upside down.

plane body

1 Tbsp (15 g)

tail wing

½ cup (100 g) · 7 in (18 cm)

1 Place 1 half sheet of nori and a ⅔ half-sheet of nori horizontally on the sushi mat and connect them at the edges with a few rice grains. Spread out ½ cup (100 g) green sushi rice in the center, about 7 in (18 cm) wide. Place the assembled plane in the center upside down. Use 1 Tbsp (15 g) green sushi rice to support the tail wing piece.

Cut small decorations from pickled yamagobo, red part of crab sticks, nori, etc., to finish.

2 Place the sushi mat on your hand and add 2½ Tbsps (40 g) green sushi rice to form a lid over the roll. Wrap the roll with the nori. Shift the roll to the edge of the sushi mat and tidy the ends. Cut into 4 equal slices. Add the decorations.

Cute Helicopters

Difficulty level ▸ ★ ★ ★ ★ ★ **Makes 4 pieces**

This is a challenging roll with lots of components, but with its bright colors and intricate detail, it's sure to delight and amaze your family and friends.

1⅔ cups (335 g) Basic Sushi Rice (see page 8), divided into:
- **Batch 1** 2¼ cups (250 g)
- **Batch 2** 3 Tbsps (45 g)
- **Batch 3** 2½ Tbsps (40 g)

For white sushi rice
Batch 1 rice
2 Tbsps (30 g) finely chopped sushi ginger
1 Tbsp toasted white sesame seeds
Mix and divide into:
½ cup (100 g)
2 x 2½ Tbsps (40 g)
2 x 2 Tbsps (30 g)
2 x 1 Tbsp (20 g)
4 x 1½ tsps (10 g)

For yellow sushi rice
Batch 2 rice
1 heaping Tbsp (20 g) Rolled Omelet (see page 19) ground to a paste
Mix and divide into:
2½ Tbsps (40 g)
2 Tbsps (25 g)

For pink sushi rice
Mix:
Batch 3
¾ tsp (5 g) oboro

Additional Ingredients
1 white kamaboko fishcake, divided (see Helicopter Body below)
4 in (10 cm) length pickled yamagobo or pickled carrot (see page 21)
2 pieces cooked kanpyo ⅜ x 4 in (1 x 10 cm)
1 piece cooked kanpyo, 2 x 4 in (5 x 10 cm), spread out and layered to make it 2 in (5 cm) wide
1 piece Rolled Omelet (see page 19) ⅜ x 1 x 4 in (1 x 3 x 10 cm)

Nori pieces

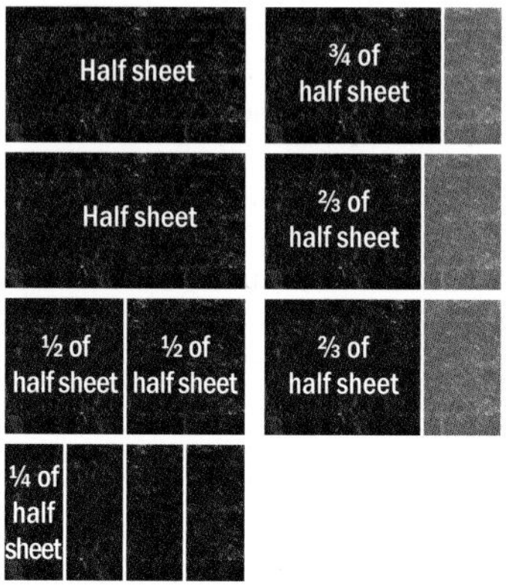

Half sheet	¾ of half sheet
Half sheet	⅔ of half sheet
½ of half sheet / ½ of half sheet	⅔ of half sheet
¼ of half sheet	

Parts

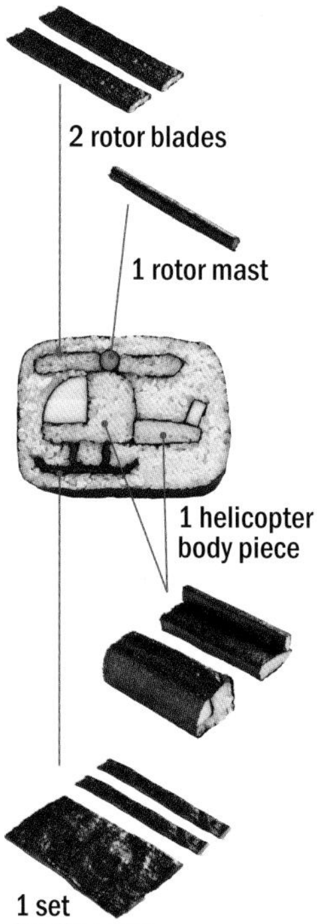

2 rotor blades

1 rotor mast

1 helicopter body piece

1 set landing skid pieces

Rotor Blades and Rotor Mast

1 half sheet nori; ¼ half-sheet nori; the pink sushi rice; 4 in (10 cm) length pickled yamagobo

1 Place the half sheet of nori on the sushi mat and spread the pink sushi rice along the center, 1¼ in (3 cm) wide. Fold the nori over the rice.

2 Cut in half across the middle. Wrap the yamagobo with the ¼ half-sheet of nori and put in the middle of the 2 halves.

Helicopter Body

¾ half-sheet nori; 2 x ½ half-sheets nori; ¼ half-sheet nori; 2½ Tbsps (40 g) yellow rice; 2 Tbsps (25 g) yellow rice; 2½ Tbsps (40 g) white rice; 2 Tbsps (30 g) white rice; 1 Tbsp (20 g) white rice; 1 piece kamaboko ⅔ x ¾ x 4 in (1.6 x 2 x 10 cm); 1 piece kamaboko ¼ x ½ x 4 in (0.5 x 1 x 10 cm); 1 piece Rolled Omelet ⅔ x 1¼ x 4 in (1 x 3 x 10 cm)

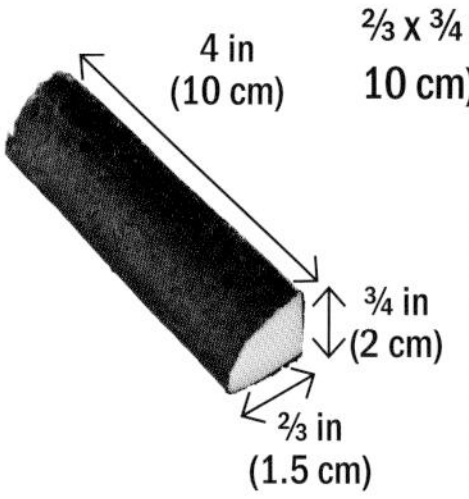

4 in (10 cm)
¾ in (2 cm)
⅔ in (1.5 cm)

2½ Tbsps (40 g)
2 Tbsps (25 g) · 1¾ in (4 cm)

1 Put the ¾ half-sheet of nori on the sushi mat and spread 2 Tbsps (25 g) yellow sushi rice in the middle 1¾ in (4 cm) wide. Wrap the large kamaboko piece on the left edge and 2½ Tbsps (40 g) yellow sushi rice to its right in a domed shape, filling in any gaps.

2 Shave about ¼ in (5 mm) off one side of the rolled omelet and wrap it with a ½ half-sheet of nori so that it is slanted a little. Wrap the small kamaboko piece with a ¼ half-sheet of nori and place it on the thin end of the omelet piece.

4 in (10 cm)
¼ in (5 mm)
⅜ in (1 cm)
1¼ in (3 cm)

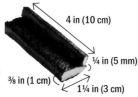

3 Place the Step 2 part on the right of the Step 1 part. Put 1 Tbsp (20 g) white sushi rice in the gap between the rolled omelet and small kamaboko pieces. Stack 2 Tbsps (30 g) white sushi rice on top and flatten.

1 Tbsp (20 g)
2 Tbsps (30 g)

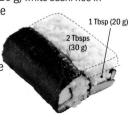

Landing Skid ⅔ half-sheet nori; 2 x ¼ half-sheets nori; 3 x 1½ tsp (10 g) portions white sushi rice; 2 small kanpyo pieces ⅜ x 4 in (1 x 10 cm); 1 large kanpyo piece 2 x 4 in (5 x 10 cm)

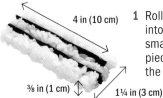

4 in (10 cm)

⅜ in (1 cm)

1¼ in (3 cm)

1 Roll the 3 portions of white sushi rice into thin sausage shapes. Wrap the small kanpyo pieces with the ¼ nori pieces and sandwich them between the rice. Form into a rectangle.

2 Wrap the large kanpyo piece with the ⅔ half-sheet of nori and drape it over the Step 1 rectangle.

Assembly

1 Put 1 half sheet of nori and a ⅔ half-sheet nori horizontally on the mat and connect them at the edges with a few rice grains. Spread ½ cup (100 g) white sushi rice in the center, 6¼ in (16 cm) wide. Put the landing skid set and 2 Tbsps (30 g) white sushi rice side by side in the center.

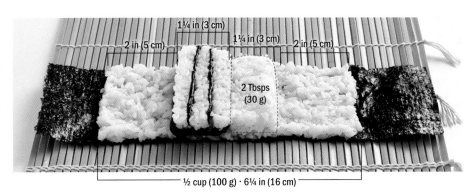

1¼ in (3 cm)

2 in (5 cm)   1¼ in (3 cm)   2 in (5 cm)

2 Tbsps (30 g)

½ cup (100 g) · 6¼ in (16 cm)

2 Place the helicopter body on top and put 1½ tsps (10 g) white sushi rice on top of the window, smoothing it so it is the same height as the helicopter body. Place the rotor set on top and put 1 Tbsp (20 g) white sushi rice to the right of the body under the rotor (its height should be shorter than the height of the small kamaboko piece).

rotor

Stack up in order.

1½ tsps (10 g)

helicopter body

landing skid

1 Tbsp (20 g)

2½ Tbsps (40 g)

3 Place the mat on your hand, and top the contents of the roll with 2½ Tbsps (40 g) white sushi rice, flattening it. Wrap the nori around to form the roll. Shift the roll to the edge of the sushi mat and tidy the ends. Cut into 4 equal slices.

PART 5

Scattered Sushi and Nigiri Sushi

Scattered sushi, called *chirashizushi* in Japanese, is the term for a bed of sushi rice topped with a variety of colorful ingredients. It is probably the easiest kind of sushi to make. *Nigiri sushi* is the type of sushi you may be most familiar with, where a small ball of rice is topped with fish or other ingredients.

Stand-out Party Pieces

The samurai fans in your life may find this traditional Samurai Helmet (page 80) just too beautiful to eat! When serving this easy-to-make scattered-sushi dish, use a black plate to make the helmet really stand out and look as though it belongs to a brave samurai warrior.

Two Types of Scattered Sushi Boxes

Difficulty levels ▶ Mt. Fuji: ★ ★ ★ Panda: ★

These scattered sushi dishes are each presented in one of the tiers of a stacking box called a jubako, which looks like a large bento box. Jubako are available online, or you can use any container about 8 inches (20 cm) square.

The key with the Mt. Fuji sushi box is to insert a layer of plastic wrap under the nigiri sushi pieces that form the lower part of the design, so that they don't stick to the layer of rice at the bottom of the box.

Mount Fuji Scattered Sushi

`For 1 box`

1⅔ cups (520 g) Basic Sushi Rice (see page 8), divided into:
  Batch 1 1¾ cups (360 g)
  Batch 2 1 Tbsp (20 g)
  Batch 3 ⅔ cup (140 g)

For the sushi rice base
Mix:
  Batch 1 rice
  1½ Tbsp chopped bettarazuke pickles
  1 tsp white sesame seeds

For black sushi rice
Mix:
  Batch 2 rice
  1 tsp ground black sesame seeds

For the nigiri sushi
Batch 3 rice divided into 7 equal portions

Additional Ingredients
1 piece smoked mackerel
4 pieces tuna sashimi
3 pieces sea bream sashimi
Small amounts of the following:
  Salmon roe; Red or orange flying fish roe; Tarako; Yukari powder; Eel (kabayaki); Squid sashimi; Nori seaweed; Cucumber; Oboro; Chopped nozawana-zuke pickles

1 Spread the sushi rice base over the bottom of the box. Spread ⅓ of the rice much thinner than the remaining ⅔.

2 Cut the smoked mackerel into a mountain shape and make 5–6 vertical cuts in it.

3 Place the mackerel on the thick part of the rice and arrange chopped nozawana-zuke pickles beneath it. Form the black sushi rice into a mountain shape on the left.

4 Scatter the top part (the "sky") with the 3 types of fish roe, starting with the tarako, then the flying fish roe, then the salmon roe. Finish the sky by scattering a small amount of yukari powder to make it appear like an evening sky. Cut the eel into shapes to form the branches of the cherry blossom tree and place the pieces to the left of the "sky."

5 Scatter the branches with cherry blossom flowers and leaves (see page 77 for instructions). To form the leaves, wrap the outside of a piece of cucumber with a piece of nori seaweed. Cut off 2 curved pieces from the outside as shown and put the cut sides together. Slice thinly to make 5 leaves.

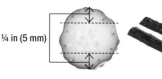

¼ in (5 mm)

6 Make the 7 pieces of nigiri sushi following the instructions on page 76. Place a layer of plastic wrap over the bed of rice before placing them in the box.

For the cherry blossom leaves, cut off the top and bottom of a nori wrapped cucumber, face together and slice finely.

Panda Scattered Sushi

2½ cups (500 g) Basic Sushi Rice (see page 8), divided into:

Batch 1 Scant 2 cups (380 g)
Batch 2 ½ cup (100 g)
Batch 3 1 heaping Tbsp (20 g)

For brown sushi rice
Mix:
Batch 1 rice
½ deep-fried tofu pocket, chopped up
1 Tbsp chopped bettarazuke pickle
1 tsp white sesame seeds

For white sushi rice
Batch 2 rice

For black sushi rice
Mix and divide into 2 equal portions:
Batch 3 rice
1 tsp ground black sesame seeds

Toppings
6–7 pieces sea bream sashimi
2 pieces salmon sashimi
2 pieces tuna sashimi
A little nori seaweed
2 thin rounds cheese kamaboko
Small amounts of the following:
salmon roe; shredded Egg Crepe
(see page 18); thinly sliced
cucumber; young bamboo leaves

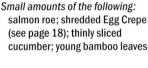

 **1** Spread the brown sushi rice evenly in the jubako box.

 **2** Form the white sushi rice into a flat disk shape and cover the top with sea bream sashimi slices.

 **3** Cut the salmon and tuna sashimi slices into half lengthwise and roll each piece into flower shapes using chopsticks.

 **4** Cover the surface of the brown rice with shredded egg crepe. Place the white sushi disk from Step 2 in the middle. Form the 2 black rice portions into ears and place them on top of the white rice disk. Cut the nori seaweed into 2 oval shapes and place on the white disk to form eye bases. Place the cheese kamaboko slices on top of the nori ovals.

 **5** Cut out the mouth and eye shapes from nori, and place as shown.

 **6** Decorate the sushi with the flowers from Step 3, salmon roe, cucumber slices and young bamboo leaves. See page 77 for a method of making cucumber leaves.

Hydrangea Flower Bowls

Difficulty level ▸ ★   `For 1 bowl`

The petals are made from bettarazuke pickles colored pink with yukari powder. The longer they stay in the coloring mix, the deeper the color will become, so adjust to your preference. See the glossary for alternative ingredient options (page 20) and coloring options (Oboro, page 21).

1 cup (200 g) Basic Sushi Rice (see page 8)

Toppings
2 pieces bettarazuke or white takuan pickles
a little lemon or yuzu zest
yukari powder
1 Tbsp white sesame seeds
1½ oz (40 g) tuna sashimi
1½ oz (40 g) salmon sashimi
¾ oz (20 g) sea bream or other white fish
   sashimi
1½ tsps sushi ginger
3 green shiso leaves

Parts

flowers

decorations

Petals   Cut 2 pieces of bettarazuke or white takuan into logs 4 x ¾ in (10 x 2 cm).

1   Cut several slivers of lemon or yuzu zest, and get ready a small bowl of yukari powder. Cut into the top of each piece of pickle as shown. Make a vertical cut first (1), then two diagonal cuts (2, 3).

2   Repeat on all 4 sides to end up with 3 cross-shaped pieces when viewed from the end.

3   Add a little water to the yukari powder and coat the pickle pieces. They will turn a light pink in about 10 minutes and a deeper pink after 40 minutes.

4 Make a whole through the center of the pickle logs with a bamboo skewer.

5 Insert several slivers of lemon or yuzu peel into the holes.

6 Slice the pickles thinly.

Assembly

1 Arrange the sushi rice on a plate in a round shape and sprinkle with the sesame seeds.

2 Dice the tuna, salmon and white fish sashimi into small pieces. Finely chop the sushi ginger. Scatter these over the sushi rice.

3 Place the green shiso leaves on top and then the pickle flowers.

4 Arrange more pickle flowers to make an attractive and balanced arrangement.

Flower Sushi

Difficulty level ▶ ★ ★   Makes 4 pieces

Learn how to make classic nigiri sushi and have fun decorating them with flowers made from simple ingredients.

① ② ③ ④

Scant ½ cup (80 g) Basic Sushi Rice (see page 8), divided into 4 equal portions of about 1 Tbsp each

Toppings

① **5-petal flower:** 1 piece sea bream sashimi; 1 piece tuna sashimi cut into 5 thin strips; a little cucumber; 1 grain salmon roe (ikura)

② **Rose:** 3 strips salmon sashimi, about ¼ – ⅓ in (5–8 mm); 1 piece sea bream sashimi; a little chervil

③ **Carnation:** 1 piece squid sashimi; 4–5 grains salmon roe (ikura); a little cucumber

④ **Cherry blossom:** 1 piece squid sashimi; 1 piece tuna sashimi; ¼ in x 2 in (5 mm x 5 cm) strip nori; a little cucumber and oboro

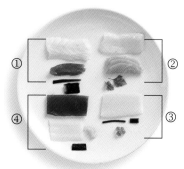

Basic Nigiri Sushi

1 Make a mixture of 3 parts rice vinegar to 7 parts water, and dip your fingertips in it.

2 Spread the vinegar water on the other hand with your moistened fingertips.

3 Take 1 tablespoon of sushi rice and press it lightly into an oval shape.

4 Put the topping on your fingers and add a little wasabi paste, if preferred.

5 Put the rice ball on top of the topping. Make a small dent in the rice ball and press both the rice and topping lightly from top and bottom.

6 Flip over so that the topping is on top. Press lightly on the sides so that the rice ball is hidden by the topping.

7 Turn the ball 180 degrees and press lightly once more to shape the sushi. The key is to use your left thumb to press the rice ball.

8 This is the completed nigiri sushi seen from the bottom. If the shape looks uneven, repeat Steps 6 and 7.

Assembly

① Five-petal Flower

1 Make small circles with the five tuna sashimi strips.

2 Make a basic nigiri sushi with sea bream sashimi. Place the tuna sashimi strips on top in a flower shape. Place a grain of salmon roe in the center. Use a thin strip of cucumber as the stem, and add 2 cucumber leaves (see page 72).

② Rose

1 Make a small cone with a piece of salmon sushi and wrap the other pieces around it to form petals.

2 Make a basic nigiri sushi using the sea bream sashimi. Put the salmon rose on top, and decorate with chervil leaves.

③ Carnation

1 Cut small, thin pieces of cucumber to make the leaves.

2 Make a basic nigiri sushi using the squid sashimi. Make a flower with grains of salmon roe. Add a thin cucumber stem and the leaves from Step 1.

④ Cherry Blossom

1 Cut each long end of the squid sashimi diagonally. Place a thin strip of nori seaweed on one edge and scatter a little oboro in the middle.

2 Fold the squid in half length-wise and cut thin slices to form the petals.

3 Make a basic nigiri sushi using the tuna sashimi. Cut 2 small squares of cucumber skin and make very fine cuts in them, leaving one edge uncut. Press lightly to spread the cut pieces into a fan shape. Place five of the petals from Step 2 on top of the tuna sushi and add the cucumber leaves.

Decorative Ball Sushi

Difficulty level ▶ ★

This type of ball-shaped sushi is called temari sushi in Japanese. A temari is a decorated ball that used to be a popular toy in Japan. These colorful and pretty sushi balls are sure to be popular with children.

1 ⅔ cup (320 g) Basic Sushi Rice (see page 8), divided into:
  Batch 1 Scant ½ cup (80 g)
  Batch 2 2¼ cups (240 g)

For 3 animal-shaped sushi pieces
Batch 1 rice, divided into:
  2 x 2 Tbsps (30 g)
  1 heaping Tbsp (20 g)

For 6 fruit-shaped sushi pieces
Batch 2 rice, divided into:
  2 x 2½ Tbsps (40 g)
  2 x 2 heaping Tbsps (35 g)
  2 x 2 Tbsps (30 g)
  1 Tbsp (20 g)
  1½ tsps (10 g)

Animal-shaped Sushi

Panda 1 piece squid sashimi 1¾ in (4 cm) square; a little nori; 2 circles pickled carrot

Form a ball with 2 Tbsps (30 g) sushi rice and the square of squid sashimi. Add the nori face parts, then small slices of yamagobo or pickled carrot for the eyes.

Rabbit 1 piece squid sashimi cut in an oval shape; 2 slivers lemon zest; 2 small pieces pickled carrot

Form a ball with the 1 heaping Tbsp sushi rice and the squid sashimi. Add lemon zest ears and yamagobo or pickled-carrot eyes.

Owl 1 thin slice scallop sashimi; tiny pieces of carrot and cucumber; nori seaweed; 2 small pieces sliced cheese

Form a ball with 2 Tbsps (30 g) sushi rice and the scallop sashimi. Add eyes and eyebrows made with the cheese kamaboko or cheese and nori. Add tiny carrot pieces to represent feathers and a cucumber beak.

Fruit Temarizushi

Decorations
① Cucumber
② Cucumber
③ Lemon
④ Cucumber
⑤ Cucumber
⑥ Green shiso leaf, cucumber

❶ Persimmon

2¾ in (7 cm) square of salmon sashimi
2 Tbsps (30 g) plain sushi rice
Small piece cucumber skin

1 Cut off the corners of the salmon sashimi. Place on a piece of cling film and top with the sushi rice formed into a ball.

2 Wrap the cling film around the salmon and rice, form into a ball, remove the cling film and turn upside down. Cut a piece of cucumber skin into a calyx and place on top of the sushi.

❷ Cherry

2 Tbsps (30 g) plain sushi rice mixed with a little oboro
Strip of cucumber skin

Mix the sushi rice with the oboro to turn it pink. Form into 2 small balls. Stick a piece of cucumber cut into a stem shape into each ball.

❸ Apple

1 x 2½ Tbsps (40 g) plain sushi rice
½ tsp aonori seaweed powder
A sliver of lemon zest

Mix the rice with the aonori to turn it green. Form into a ball, and make a small dent in the top. Cut the sliver of lemon zest into a stem and insert into the dent.

❹ Orange

1 heaping Tbsp (35 g) plain sushi rice
½ tsp red-orange flying fish roe
Small piece of cucumber skin

Mix the rice with the fish roe to turn the rice orange. Form into a slightly flattened ball. Cut a thin slice of cucumber into a leaf shape and put on top of the ball.

❺ Peach

2 Tbsps (30 g) plain sushi rice mixed with 1 tsp oboro
1½ tsps (10 g) plain sushi rice mixed with ½ tsp tarako
Small piece cucumber skin

Form the light pink sushi rice into a ball. Put the darker pink sushi rice on top to create a gradient effect. Form into a peach shape. Add cut into leaf shapes.

❻ Strawberry

1 heaping Tbsp (35 g) plain sushi rice
½ tsp pickled plum paste
A few white sesame seeds
1 green shiso leaf
A sliver of cucumber

Mix the rice, plum paste and sesame seeds, and form into a strawberry shape. Fold a green shiso leaf in half lengthwise and cut into a V shape, as shown. Make a hole in the shiso leaf with a skewer and secure it to the strawberry with a sliver of cucumber.

❼ Chestnut

1 x 2½ Tbsps (40 g) plain sushi rice
A little chicken soboro (see page 20)
A few ground black sesame seeds

Mix the rice with the chicken. Form into a chestnut shape and dip the rounded end into the sesame seeds.

Samurai Helmet

Difficulty level ▸ ★ ★   [Makes 1 helmet]

This fun decorative sushi is the perfect treat for
anyone who loves samurai! Use the templates
on the facing page to shape the helmet parts.

Scant 1 cup (180 g) Basic Sushi Rice (see page 8), divided into:
Batch 1 ½ cup (100 g)
Batch 2 3 Tbsps (50 g)
Batch 3 2 Tbsps (30 g)

For white sushi rice
Batch 1 rice
1 tsp white sesame seeds
Mix and divide into:
    2 x 2 Tbsp (30 g)
    2 x 1 heaping Tbsp (20 g)

For black sushi rice
Mix:
    Batch 2 rice
    1 tsp ground black sesame seeds

For green sushi rice
Mix:
    Batch 3 rice
    1 tsp finely chopped nozawana-zuke
    A few white sesame seeds

Toppings
3 square slices kamaboko fish cake
2 pieces Rolled Omelet (see page 19),
    4¾ x 2 x ⅜ in (12 x 5 x 1 cm)
2 slices tuna sashimi, cut into squares
1 salmon sashimi, cut into thin strips
⅓ sheet nori seaweed
2 sprigs mitsuba or flat leaf parsley, blanched
1 thin slice pickled yamagobo or pickled carrot
    (see page 21)
a little salmon roe (ikura)

Parts

Cut out or form the components using the
templates on the facing page.

rolled omelet

Black sushi rice

2 pieces kamaboko

Assembly

1 Arrange the black sushi rice,
green sushi rice and the
two 2 Tbsp (30 g) portions of
white sushi rice as shown in the
photo.

2 Place the square kamaboko
pieces on top of the white sushi
rice and put the 1 heaping Tbsp
(20 g) white sushi rice portions on
either side of the black sushi rice.

3 Place the omelet kuwagata
crest in the center as shown.
Place the square tuna pieces on
top of the fukigaeshi side pieces
and the salmon strips around the
oval green sushi.

4 Cut out the nori sheet and place on top of the black sushi rice. Decorate the fukigaeshi side pieces with sort lengths of mitsuba stem.

5 Place 2 more pieces of mitsuba stem along the edges of the nori on the black sushi rice. Decorate with the yamagobo circle, small squares of kamaboko and a spoonful of salmon roe. Line the edges of the fukigaeshi side pieces with strips of nori and top with squares of kamaboko. Finish by tying the remaining mitsuba sprig into a bow and placing it under the helmet.

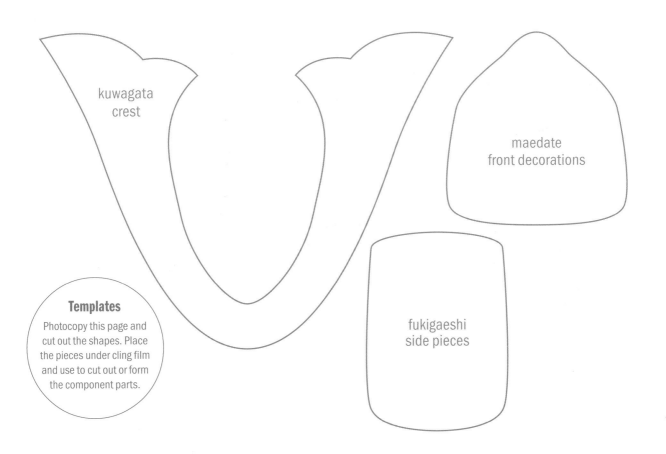

kuwagata crest

maedate front decorations

fukigaeshi side pieces

Templates

Photocopy this page and cut out the shapes. Place the pieces under cling film and use to cut out or form the component parts.

PART 6

Sushi for Special Occasions

This chapter presents a selection of recipes for sushi rolls that are perfect for celebrations or special days. These beautiful creations will make your dinner party or any other occasion instantly festive.

It's a Celebration!

March 3 is the Doll Festival in Japan, known as Hina Matsuri. Families with young daughters make displays that represent the emperor, empress and the imperial court. You can make the sushi for this beautiful display by following the recipe for Doll Sushi Rolls on page 86.

Both the crane and the turtle are symbols of good luck and longevity in Japanese folklore, so these sushi rolls are ideal for celebrating significant birthdays. You'll find the recipe for Lucky Cranes on page 88, and for Lucky Turtles on page 90.

Rosette Messages

Difficulty level ▸ ★ `Makes 4 rosettes`

Bright and colorful, these rosettes are easy to make. The ones here use the Japanese words "Back to School" (left) and "Congratulations," (right) but you can use other words to suit any celebratory occasion.

For pink sushi rice
Mix:
  2½ Tbsps (40 g) Basic Sushi Rice (see page 8)
  1½ tsps (10 g) oboro

Additional Ingredients
2 pieces Egg Crepe (see page 18), each 4 x 7½ in (10 x 19 cm)
A little shredded pickled red ginger or other red ingredient
  (tarako, mentaiko, etc.)
2 crab sticks
1 block kamaboko fish cake, 4 x 1¾ x 1 in (10 x 4 x 2.5 cm)

Nori pieces

| Half sheet | ¾ of half sheet | use the rest to form words |

Parts

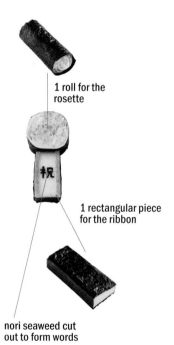

1 roll for the rosette

1 rectangular piece for the ribbon

nori seaweed cut out to form words

Rosette   ¾ half-sheet nori; pink sushi rice; 2 pieces egg crepe, cut as above; red pickled ginger

1 Place the 2 sheets of egg crepe side by side. Scatter with small clumps of pink sushi rice. Scatter red pickled ginger shreds between the sushi rice clumps.

2 Roll up 1 egg crepe, then roll the other over the first crepe to form 1 roll.

3 Roll the nori piece over the rolled egg crepes.

4 Tidy the ends and then cut the roll into 4 evenly sized pieces.

Ribbon **1 half sheet nori; 2 crab sticks; 1 block kamaboko fish cake, cut as below**

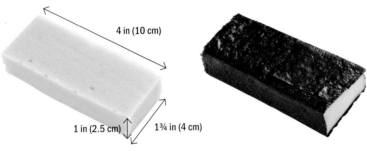

4 in (10 cm)

1 in (2.5 cm)   1¾ in (4 cm)

1 Cut the kamaboko into a rectangle roughly the same size as shown.

2 Wrap the kamaboko in the piece of nori.

⅔ in (1.5 cm)

3 Slice into ⅔ in (1.5 cm) wide pieces, a little thinner than the rosette. A 4-in (10 cm) block will yield about 6 pieces.

Assembly

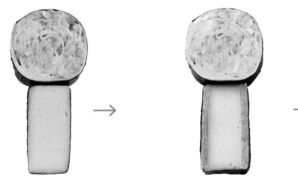

→

→

1 Place the rosette and the ribbon as shown.

2 Put thin strips of the red part of the crab sticks on either side of the ribbon.

3 Decorate with the words cut out of nori.

Doll Sushi Rolls

Difficulty level ▶ ★ ★ `Makes 4 pieces`

Hina dolls are put up on March 3, Girls' Day or the Doll Festival in Japan, but you can use this pretty sushi for any occasion. Add ladies-in-waiting and court musicians to make the festive display shown on page 83.

1 cup (215 g) Basic Sushi Rice (see page 8), divided into:

Batch 1 ⅓ cup (75 g)	**Batch 3** 3 Tbsps (50 g)
Batch 2 3 Tbsps (50 g)	**Batch 4** 2½ Tbsps (40 g)

For white sushi rice
Batch 1 rice

For black sushi rice
Mix:
 Batch 2 rice
 1 Tbsp ground black sesame
  seeds
 ½ tsp yukari powder

For green sushi rice
Mix:
 Batch 3 rice
 1 tsp finely chopped pickles
 ⅓ tsp aonori powder

For pink sushi rice
Mix:
 Batch 4 rice
 1½ tsps (10 g) oboro

Additional Ingredients
4 pieces cucumber, ¾ in (2 cm) in length
2 pieces Rolled Omelet (see page 19),
 1¼ x 4 in (3 x 10 cm)
a little kamaboko fish cake

Ladies-in-Waiting and Musicians
See ingredients on facing page

Nori pieces

Half sheet

½ of half sheet

⅓ of half sheet

2¾ in (7 cm) 2¾ in (7 cm)

use the leftovers to make eyes and mouths

Parts

1 hair roll

2 crowns

2 crowns

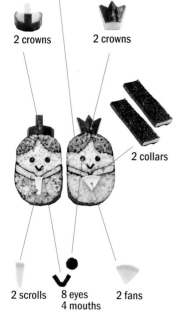

2 collars

2 scrolls   8 eyes / 4 mouths   2 fans

Hair Roll   ½ half-sheet nori; black sushi rice

1 Place the ½ half-sheet of nori on the sushi mat. Form the rice into a sausage shape and place in the middle of the nori. Roll.

2 Cut the roll in half lengthwise.

Collars
2 pieces nori, each 2¾ in (7 cm) wide
2 pieces Rolled Omelet (see page 19)

1 Cut the omelet pieces as shown, so that the sides are slanted.

2 Wrap the 2 cut omelet blocks with nori.

Prince's Crown   2 pieces cucumber, ¾ in (2 cm) long

Cut one side off the cucumber as shown in the 1st photo, then cut into the remaining piece leaving the center. Make two crowns.

Princess's Crown   2 pieces cucumber, ¾ in (2 cm) long

Cut off both sides of the cucumber, then cut the top part into a crown shape as shown. Make two crowns.

Assembly

1¼ in (3 cm)   1¼ in (3 cm)

1 Connect the half sheet and ⅓ half-sheet of nori with a few grains of sushi rice, and place on the sushi mat. Place the 2 hair roll halves in the middle with the cut sides facing down.

2 Place the white sushi rice on top of the two roll halves, leaving no gaps. Form the top into a triangular shape, and place the collar parts on top in an inverted V shape.

3 Place the sushi mat on your hand. Fill half with the green sushi rice and the other half with the pink sushi rice.

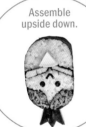

Assemble upside down.

4 Press the sushi rice to the edge of the roll, tidy the ends and cut the roll into 4 pieces.

5 Finish by adding the eyes, mouths, crowns, scroll and fan.

→

Ladies-in-Waiting and Musicians

1 whole sheet nori; ¾ cup (150 g) basic sushi rice; 4 in (10 cm) strips of cucumber and maguro tuna

Place a whole nori sheet on a sushi mat so that the long side is horizontal. Spread the sushi rice on the nori and place the cucumber strip on one side and the tuna strip on the other as shown. Roll the sushi in a spiral (rolling in the nori), and end by pressing it into a triangular shape. Flatten the bottom and cut the roll into **10 even pieces**. Add eyes and mouths with leftover ingredients, if desired, and arrange with the prince and princess hina doll sushi pieces.

Lucky Cranes

Difficulty level ▶ ★ ★ ★ ★ ★ **Makes 4 pieces**

The crane, considered to be a very lucky symbol in Japan, is noted for the graceful shape of its neck. When assembling this challenging sushi roll, pay particular attention to the width and curve of the crane's neck.

1½ cups + 1 Tbsp (315 g) Basic Sushi Rice (see page 8), divided into:
   Batch 1 Scant 1 cup (180 g)
   Batch 2 just over ½ cup (120 g)
   Batch 3 1 Tbsp (15 g)

For red sushi rice
Batch 1 rice
1 Tbsp (20 g)
   mentaiko
Mix and divide into:
   ½ cup (100 g)
   Scant ½ cup (80 g)
   1 Tbsp (15 g)
   ¾ tsp (5 g)

For white sushi rice
Batch 2 rice, divided into:
   Scant ½ cup (80 g)
   2 Tbsps (30 g)
   1½ tsps (10 g)

For black sushi rice
Mix:
   Batch 3 rice
   ½ tsp ground sesame seeds

Additional Ingredients
4 in (10 cm) length
   pickled yamagobo
   or pickled carrot (see
   p. 21), halved lengthwise
4 in (10 cm) length
   cucumber, halved
   lengthwise
4 black sesame seeds

Nori pieces

| Half sheet | Half sheet |

⅔ of half sheet | ⅓ of half sheet | ½ of half sheet | use the rest for the wings

1¾ in (4 cm)

Parts

1 head and neck piece

1 bill piece

4 eye pieces

1 wing piece

Head and Neck
Half sheet nori; 1¾ in (4 cm) wide nori piece; 2 Tbsps (30 g) white sushi rice, 1½ tsps (10 g) white sushi rice; black sushi rice; pickled yamagobo

slants diagonally   ¾ in (2 cm)   ⅜ in (1 cm)
1½ tsps (10 g)   2 Tbsps (30 g)

1 Place the half sheet of nori on the sushi matt, then the yamagobo piece in the center with the cut (flat) side facing down. Spread the 1½ tsp (10 g) portion of white sushi rice on top of the yamagobo so it slants diagonally to one side. Leave a ¾ in (2 cm) wide gap on the nori, and spread the 2 Tbsp (30 g) portion of white sushi rice so it slants up as shown. Leave a ⅜ in (1 cm) gap at the edge of the nori.

2 Spread the black sushi rice evenly on the 1¾ in (4 cm) wide nori piece.

3 Place the Step 2 part on the Step 1 piece between the two white rice mounds, the rice facing up, and press down lightly to form a dent. Pull the left side of the nori over the rice and press on the other side to close, as shown in the photo above.

 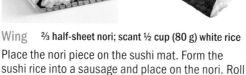 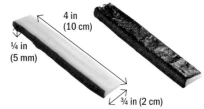

4 in (10 cm)
¼ in (5 mm)
¾ in (2 cm)

Wing   ⅔ half-sheet nori; scant ½ cup (80 g) white rice

Place the nori piece on the sushi mat. Form the sushi rice into a sausage and place on the nori. Roll into a rounded triangle shape.

Beak   ⅓ half-sheet nori; cucumber piece

Cut the cucumber piece into a triangular shape ¼ x ¾ x 4 in (0.5 x 2 x 10 cm). Pat dry and wrap with the nori.

Assembly

1 Place the head and neck piece so that the yamagobo is on the left upper side. Place the beak part to the left of the yamagobo with the thin end facing outwards. Use ¾ tsp (5 g) of red sushi rice to hold the two pieces together.

2 Line the sushi mat with cling film. Place the piece from Step 1 on it and form into an S shape as shown.

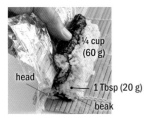

3 Place the piece vertically with the beak part on the bottom as shown. Peel the cling film off one side and put the scant ½ cup (80 g) of red sushi rice on the piece. If you put 1 heaping Tbsp (20 g) of this red rice in the dent between the neck and the beak first, it is easier to put on the remaining ¼ cup (60 g) of red rice.

4 Connect the remaining half sheet of nori and the ½ half-sheet of nori with a few rice grains and place on the sushi mat. Place the Step 3 part (the head) to the left of the center point as shown.

5 Put the wing part on the right side of the head piece and add 1 Tbsp (15 g) red sushi rice in between the pieces.

Stack up in order.

beak

head and neck

wing

6 Place the ½ cup (100 g) red sushi rice on top of the pieces. Form a square shape using the sushi mat in one hand and shaping with the other.

7 Transfer the roll to the edge of the sushi mat and tidy up the shape. Cut into 4 even pieces.

8 Add black sesame seeds as eyes and thinly cut some nori pieces for the wings.

Lucky Turtles

Difficulty level ▶ ★ ★ ★ ★ **Makes 4 pieces**

The turtle is another lucky animal in Japanese folklore. The key here is to make sure the head of the turtle tilts upwards. Also take care not to make the legs too long, otherwise the turtle will look unbalanced.

Scant 1½ cups (285 g) Basic Sushi Rice (see page 8), divided into:
Batch 1 1 cup (200 g)
Batch 2 Scant ½ cup (85 g)

For white sushi rice
Batch 1 rice
A little sushi ginger, finely chopped
1 tsp toasted white sesame seeds
Mix and divide into:
   Scant ½ cup (80 g)
   ¼ cup (60 g)
   1 heaping Tbsp (20 g)
   2 x Tbsps (15 g)
   2 x 1½ tsps (10 g)

For green sushi rice
Batch 2 rice
1½ tsps (10 g) green flying fish roe
1 tsp aonori powder
Mix and divide into:
   3 x 1 Tbsp (15 g)
   5 x 1½ tsps (10 g)

Additional Ingredients
4 in (10 cm) length cheese kamaboko
4 in (10 cm) length fish sausage

Nori pieces

use for the eyes

Parts

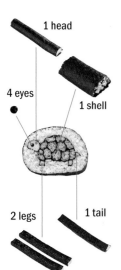

1 head

1 shell

4 eyes

2 legs

1 tail

Shell 5 x ¼ half-sheets nori; 3 x ⅓ half-sheets nori; 1 x ¾ half-sheet nori;
5 x 1½ tsps (10 g) green sushi rice; 3 x 1 Tbsp (15 g) portions green sushi rice

1 Place one ¼ half-sheet of nori on the sushi mat. Form 1½ tsps (10 g) of the green sushi rice into a thin sausage. Place on the nori and roll into a thin (A) roll. Make 4 (A) rolls. Repeat with the ⅓ half-sheets of nori and the 1 Tbsp (15 g) green sushi rice portions to make 3 fatter (B) rolls.

2 Cut the fatter (B) rolls in half lengthwise once the nori has softened.

3 Put the ¾ half-sheet of nori on the mat. Put the halved (B) rolls in the center and cut sides down.

2 rolls

4 Put 2 of the (A) rolls on top.

put on 3 rolls

5 Holding the sushi mat in your hand to form a half-moon shape, put the 3 other (A) rolls on top and form the whole roll into a dome shape.

Slice off ⅓ of the cheese lengthwise.
Wrap the nori around the remaining ⅔ .

Cut the fish sausage into 4 strips ¼ in (5 mm) long and 1 triangular
strip of the same dimensions. Wrap each strip in the nori.

Assembly

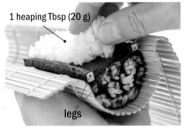

1 heaping Tbsp (20 g)

legs

1 Holding the sushi mat in one hand, place the shell piece on it, rounded
side facing down. Holding it in a rounded shape, place a leg piece on each
edge and 1 heaping Tbsp (20 g) white sushi rice in the middle. Set aside.

2 Stick a half sheet of nori and a ½ half-sheet of nori together with rice grains.
Place on the sushi mat. Spread the scant ½ cup (80 g) white sushi rice on the
nori in the middle and spread 6¼ in (16 cm) wide. Place the piece assembled in
Step 1 on top, rounded side up. Top with 1 Tbsp (15 g) white sushi rice and the head
piece, tilted at an angle. Top the head piece with 1½ tsps (10 g) white sushi rice. Put
1½ tsps (10 g) white sushi rice on the right side of the Step 1 piece and top with the
tail piece, one flat side facing inwards. Top with 1 Tbsp (15 g) white rice.

Stack up in order.

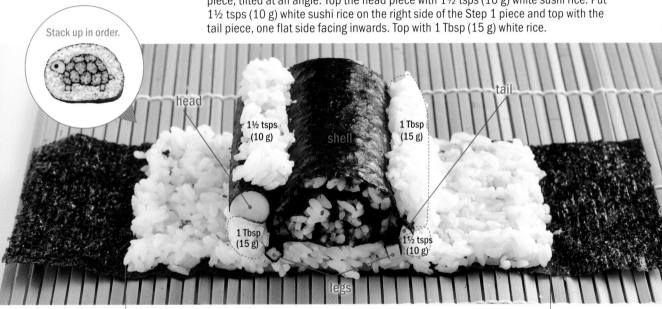

head

tail

1½ tsps
(10 g)

shell

1 Tbsp
(15 g)

1 Tbsp
(15 g)

1½ tsps
(10 g)

legs

Scant ½ cup (80 g) · 6¼ in (16 cm)

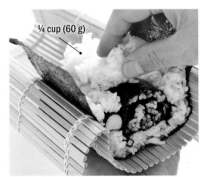

¼ cup (60 g)

4 Transfer the roll to the sushi mat, tidy up
the shape and cut into 4 even pieces.

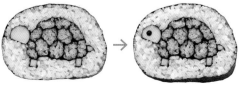

3 Hold the sushi mat in one hand in a
rounded shape. Top with ¼ cup (60 g)
white sushi rice and form the roll.

5 Add eyes with the
leftover nori.

New Year's Lions

Difficulty level ▶ ★ ★ ★ ★ ★   **Makes 4 pieces**

The shishimai lion dance is performed at New Year in Japan, to bring good luck. For a scattered sushi version of this sushi roll, see page 94.

1½ cups (300 g) Basic Sushi Rice (see page 8), divided into:
Batch 1 Scant 1 cup (180 g)   **Batch 3** 2½ Tbsps (40 g)
Batch 2 ¼ cup (60 g)   **Batch 4** 1 heaping Tbsp (20 g)

For green sushi rice
Batch 1 rice
1½ tsps (10 g) finely chopped
    nozawana-zuke pickle stems
1½ tsps (10 g) green flying fish roe
1 tsp aonori powder
Mix and divide into:
    ½ cup (100 g)
    2½ Tbsps (40 g)
    2 x 2 Tbsps (30 g)

For red sushi rice
Batch 2 rice
1 Tbsp (15 g) mentaiko
Mix and divide into:
    2 Tbsps (30 g)
    3 x 1 Tbsp (15 g) portions

For black sushi rice
Mix and divide into 2 equal portions:
    Batch 3 rice
    1 tsp ground black sesame seeds
    ½ tsp yukari powder

For white sushi rice
Batch 4 rice, divided into 4 equal portions

Additional Ingredients
Kamaboko fish cake, 4 x 1¾ x ⅔ in (10 x 4 x 1.5 cm)
4 in (10 cm) length cheese kamaboko
1 slice processed cheese
a few black sesame seeds

Nori pieces

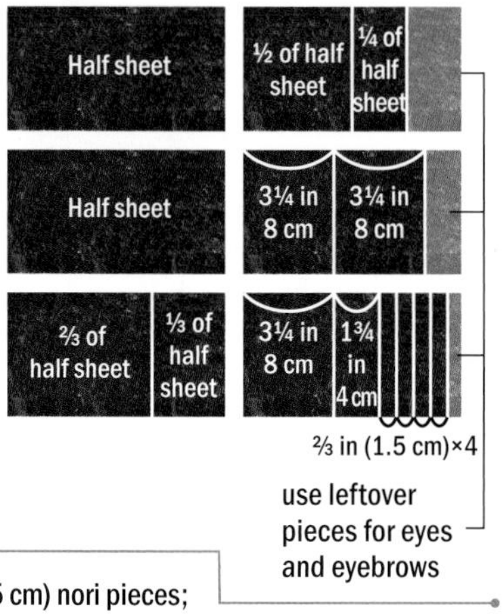

Half sheet	½ of half sheet	¼ of half sheet
Half sheet	3¼ in 8 cm	3¼ in 8 cm
⅔ of half sheet	⅓ of half sheet	3¼ in 8 cm	1¾ in 4 cm

⅔ in (1.5 cm)×4

use leftover pieces for eyes and eyebrows

Parts

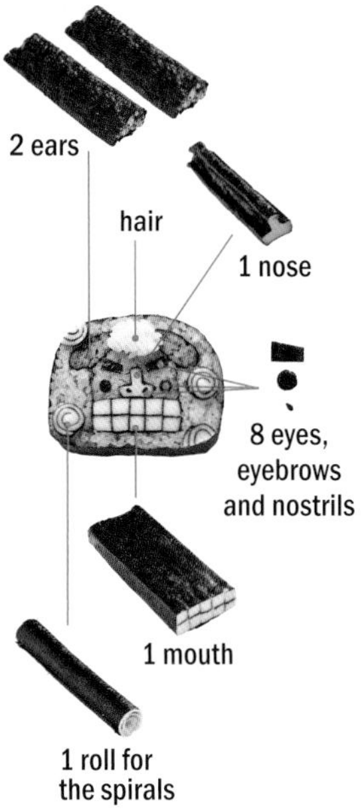

2 ears

hair

1 nose

8 eyes, eyebrows and nostrils

1 mouth

1 roll for the spirals

Mouth   ⅔ half-sheet nori; 1¾ in (4 cm) nori piece; 4 x ½ in (1.5 cm) nori pieces; 1 rectangular white kamaboko fish cake

1¾ in (4 cm)   4 in (10 cm)
⅔ in (1.5 cm)

1 Cut the kamaboko into 1¾ x ⅔ x 4 in (4 x 1.5 x 10 cm). Split in half lengthwise and sandwich the 1½ in (4 cm) nori piece in between.

2 Cut this into 5 equal sized strips. Reassemble into a rectangle with the ⅔ in (1.5 cm) nori pieces sandwiched between the strips. Wrap the whole rectangle with the ⅔ nori piece.

Nose   ⅓ nori piece; 4 in (10 cm) cheese kamaboko

Cut off ⅓ of the cheese kamaboko as shown in the 1st picture. With the cut side down, cut the top as shown in the 2nd picture. Wrap the cut piece in the nori.

Spirals   3¼ in (8 cm) nori piece; cheese slice

Place the cheese slice on the nori piece. Roll it into a spiral shape from the near side. Secure the end edge with a few rice grains. Slice into 12 thin pieces.

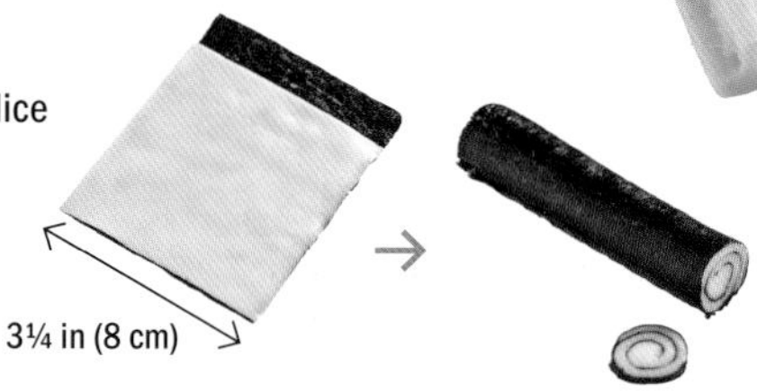

3¼ in (8 cm)

Ears   2 x 3¼ in (8 cm) nori pieces; 2 portions black sushi rice

Place a nori piece on the sushi mat. Spread 1 portion of the rice in the middle, about 1¼ in (3 cm) wide. Fold the nori over the rice and form the whole into a teardrop shape. Make 2.

Lion Head Half sheet nori ; ¼ half-sheet nori; red sushi rice, portioned as in ingredients list; mouth, ear and nose pieces

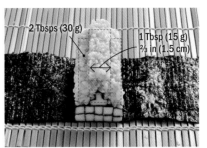

1 Connect the half sheet of nori and ¼ half-sheet of nori with a few rice grains and place on the mat. Place the mouth and nose pieces in the center.

2 Put 1 Tbsp (15 g) red sushi rice on each side of the nose piece.

3 Place 2 Tbsps (30 g) red sushi rice on top and smooth it out into a triangular shape. Flatten the top and place 1 Tbsp (15 g) of red sushi rice on top. Form into a ⅔ in (1.5 cm) wide rectangle.

4 Hold the sushi mat in your hand while squeezing the contents from both sides. Place the ear pieces on the left and right with the thick parts facing outwards. Place them so that half of each ear is on the flaps of the sushi mat. Roll the whole rather loosely so that the ears point downwards.

5 Flip the whole over, holding onto the face part to make it square. Press the head roll all around so that the nori adheres well to the rice inside.

Assembly

mouth
nose
2 Tbsps (30 g)
2 Tbsps (30 g)
ear

Assemble upside down.

½ cup (100 g) · 6¾ in (17 cm)

1 Connect a half sheet of nori and a ½ half-sheet of nori with a few rice grains and place on the sushi mat. Spread ½ cup (100 g) green sushi rice in the middle, 6¾ in (17 cm) wide. Place the assembled head roll upside down in the middle. Place 2 Tbsps (30 g) green sushi rice on both sides of the head.

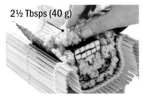

2½ Tbsps (40 g)

2 Put the sushi mat on your hand, cupping the roll. Spread 2½ Tbsps (40 g) green sushi rice evenly on top.

3 Transfer the roll to the edge of the sushi mat, tidy the shape and cut into 4 equal pieces. Add nori eyebrows and eyes and black sesame seed nostrils. Put some white sushi rice in between the ears to represent the hair. Place the spiral slices on the green sushi rice, cutting into half when needed.

It is fine if the mouth gets a bit twisted. The lion will look fierce!

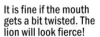

A Lion Dance Scene

Difficulty level ▸ ★ ★ ★   `Makes 1 plate`

This scattered sushi with a lion dance theme makes use of the sushi roll from the page 92, sliced into 6 pieces rather than 4. For an extra layer of taste and interest, try adding some Rolled Omelet (page 19) or salmon roe under the green sushi rice!

Nori pieces

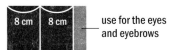

use for the eyes and eyebrows

1¾ cups (360 g) Basic Sushi Rice (see page 8), divided into:
Batch 1 1⅔ cups (320 g)
Batch 2 2½ Tbsps (40 g)

For green sushi rice
Mix and divide into 6 equal portions:
Batch 1 rice
1 heaping Tbsp (20 g) finely chopped nozawana-zuke stems
1 heaping Tbsp (20 g) green flying fish roe
1½ tsps aonori seaweed

For white sushi rice
Batch 2 rice divided into 6 equal portions

Additional Ingredients
Rolled Omelet (page 19), to taste
Salmon roe (ikura), to taste
* For 6 servings (not including the sushi rolls)

Parts

2 rolls for the spirals

12 eyebrows, eyes, nostrils

1 head

Assembly

1 Make the New Year's Lion roll on pages 92–93. Cut into 6 equal pieces. (For standalone sushi rolls, cut the roll into 4 equal pieces.)

2 Place a couple of rolled omelet slices on a small plate and scatter with some salmon roe. Top with one portion green sushi rice formed into a flat disk. Add a slice of the Shishimai Sushi Roll, then use the nori to make the eyebrows, eyes and nostrils. Top with white sushi rice to form the hair. Repeat this process 6 times.

3 Scatter with spiral rolls (see page 92). Place the New Year's Pine Tree sushi (see facing page) on each side.

New Year's Pine Trees

Difficulty level ▸ ★ 〔Makes 2 pieces〕

This is a traditional New Year Shinto decoration that is put on either side of the entrance to a house to attract good luck. The decoration goes well with the Lion Dance Scene on the facing page. Asparagus is easy to work with and can make a perfectly matching pair.

For brown sushi rice
Mix:
2 Tbsps (30 g) Basic Sushi Rice (see page 8)
1½ tsps (10 g) chicken soboro (see page 20)

Additional Ingredients
3 straight green asparagus stalks
a little mayonnaise
a little looseleaf lettuce
2 long flat leaf parsley stems, blanched briefly
1 thin slice pink kamaboko fish cake
a little salmon roe

Nori pieces

2¾ in (7 cm)
1¼ in (3 cm)   5 in (13 cm)

Parts

1 bamboo

1 decoration

1 container

Bamboo   1 x 1¼ in (3 cm) wide nori piece; 1 x 6 in (15 cm) length asparagus; 2 x 5 in (13 cm) length asparagus

6 in (15 cm)   5 in (13 cm)   5 in (13 cm)

1 Boil the asparagus stalks in salted water, and cut to the measurements on the left.

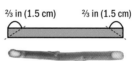

⅔ in (1.5 cm)   ⅔ in (1.5 cm)

2 Cut both ends of all 3 pieces diagonally as shown, about ⅔ in (1.5 cm) long.

3 Line up the 3 pieces so that the cut sides are facing the same way. Wrap the middle with the nori piece, securing it with a few rice grains.

Container   1 nori piece, 2¾ x 5 in (7 x 13 cm); 2½ Tbsps (40 g) brown sushi rice

1 Place the nori piece on the sushi mat as shown, and spread the brown sushi rice evenly over it.

2 Reserve the rice spread nori piece on a cutting board. Spread a little mayonnaise on both sides, leaving a little blank space. Place a small piece of loose leaf lettuce on the edges with the frilly edges sticking out.

Assembly

1 Place the asparagus on top of the nori as shown.

2 Wrap from the near side. Wrap in cling film, rest for a bit until the nori has become a little moist, then cut in half.

3 Take the cling film off, stand each piece upright and wrap with the blanched mitsuba or flatleaf parsley. Decorate with small pieces of kamaboko cut into fan shapes and salmon roe.

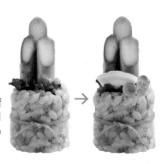

Books to Span the East and West

Our core mission at Tuttle Publishing is to create books which bring people together one page at a time. Tuttle was founded in 1832 in the small New England town of Rutland, Vermont (USA). Our fundamental values remain as strong today as they were then—to publish best-in-class books informing the English-speaking world about the countries and peoples of Asia. The world is a smaller place today and Asia's economic, cultural and political influence has expanded, yet the need for meaningful dialogue and information about this diverse region has never been greater. Since 1948, Tuttle has been a leader in publishing books on the cultures, arts, cuisines, languages and literatures of Asia. Our authors and photographers have won many awards and Tuttle has published thousands of titles on subjects ranging from martial arts to paper crafts. We welcome you to explore the wealth of information available on Asia at www.tuttlepublishing.com.

Published by Tuttle Publishing, an imprint of Periplus Editions (HK) Ltd.

www.tuttlepublishing.com

KAWASUMI KEN NO ICHIBAN OISHI! KAZARI MAKIZUSHI & KAZARI CHIRASHIZUSHI NO TSURIKATA
Copyright © Ken Kawasumi 2015
English translation rights arranged with SHUFUNOTOMO CO., LTD
through Japan UNI Agency, Inc., Tokyo

English translation ©2020 Periplus Editions (HK) Ltd. English translation by Makiko Itoh.

ISBN 978-4-8053-1590-3

First edition
23 22 21 20   8 7 6 5 4 3 2 1
2009EP

Printed in Singapore

TUTTLE PUBLISHING® is a registered trademark of Tuttle Publishing, a division of Periplus Editions (HK) Ltd.

Distributed by

North America, Latin America & Europe
Tuttle Publishing
364 Innovation Drive
North Clarendon, VT 05759-9436 U.S.A.
Tel: 1 (802) 773-8930
Fax: 1 (802) 773-6993
info@tuttlepublishing.com
www.tuttlepublishing.com

Japan
Tuttle Publishing
Yaekari Building, 3rd Floor, 5-4-12 Osaki
Shinagawa-ku, Tokyo 141 0032
Tel: (81) 3 5437-0171
Fax: (81) 3 5437-0755
sales@tuttle.co.jp
www.tuttle.co.jp

Asia Pacific
Berkeley Books Pte Ltd
3 Kallang Sector #04-01
Singapore 349278
Tel: (65) 6741 2178
Fax: (65) 6741 2179
inquiries@periplus.com.sg
www.tuttlepublishing.com